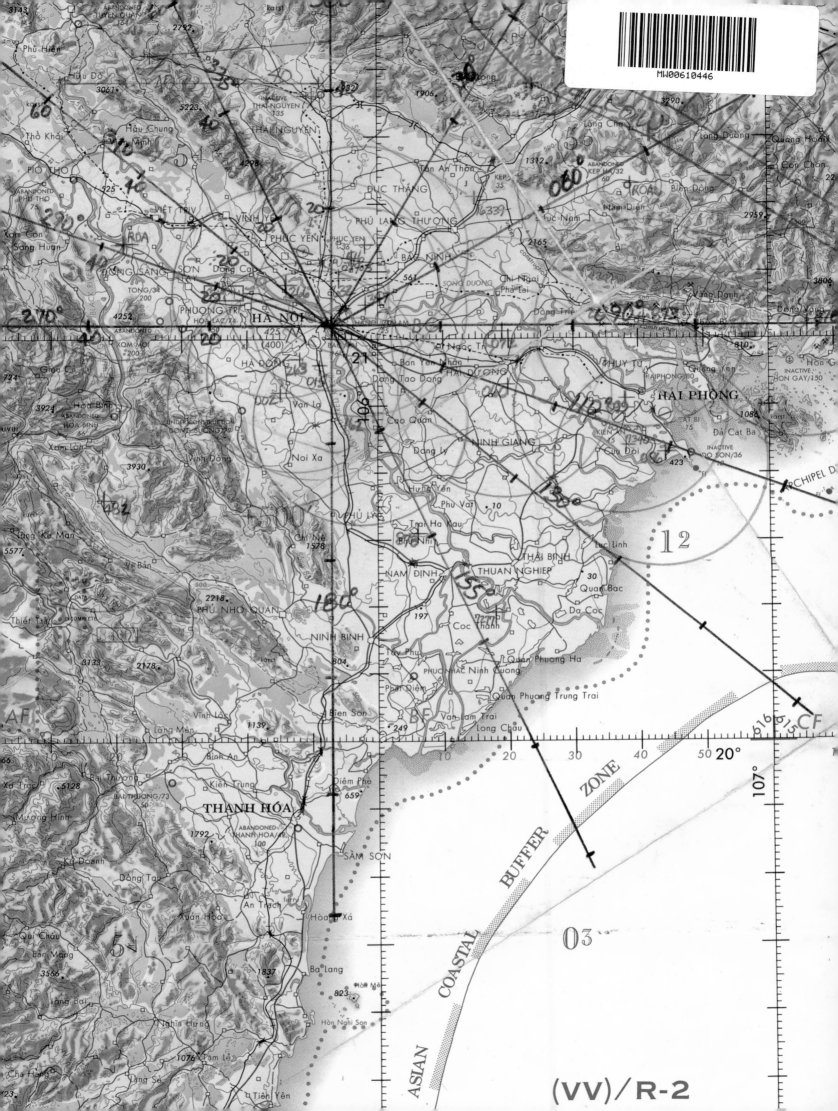

(VV)/R-2

Roll Call: THUD

A Photographic Record of the F-105 Thunderchief

Roll Call: THUD

A Photographic Record of the F-105 Thunderchief

John M. Campbell & Michael Hill

Schiffer Military/Aviation History
Atglen, PA

ACKNOWLEDGEMENTS

John and I gratefully acknowledge the help and support of the following individuals and organizations in this project.

Special mention to Colonel Jack Broughton, author of THUD RIDGE and GOING DOWNTOWN, for writing the foreword and loaning photos for this project. Your "SPITTEN KITTENS" are doing well.

Thanks to W.H. Plunkett for opening his database on the THUD to us. Without his help we would not have as much of the information on the individual aircraft as we do. We have come to call him PAPPA THUD.

Special Thanks to Marty Isham and Paul Minert for opening their collections of photos to our use.

Robert D. Archer for the filling of many gaps in the role call through his collection of material.

Charles Byler for his photos and information on the 36th TFW at Bitburg.

William Malerba for his gap filling loan of photos. It was very welcome.

Kim Pepperill for the use of photos and his "special map" of Route Pak 6.

Mr. John Davis and the staff of the Kansas Aeronautical History Society.

THANKS to the following for the loan of photos, material and support: Jeff Ethel, Steve "Poker Bear" Meyerson, Gene Fitzharris, Don Logan, Joe Bruch, Paul "CoolBear" Chesley, Charles Mayer, Jerry Geer, William Reid Dale Messimer, Jerry Kochman, Jerry Arruda, DonSpering, Paul Hoynacki, Hugh Muir, Paul Paulson, Barry Miller, Steve Miller, C.D. Snyder, Paul Metz Don Truax, Paul Swendrowski, Jim Rotramel, Fred Keuykendal Jr, Capt. Rich Curry 507th TFS, Whitey Blanchard, Col. John "Iron Duke" Russell, Mandy Humphries, David James and Steve Brown, Steve and Mary Bowers, Dorothy Campbell, Jim Green, and Frank Strnad.

We must also THANK Dr. James Crowder, Dr. Donald Klinko, and Laura Casey at the Tinker AFB History Office for their help.

John and I also wish to THANK Peter Schiffer and Bob Biondi of Schiffer Publishing for their interest, support, and patience in this project.

Special thanks also to John Heyer for his photographic contributions, many of which are uncredited.

Special Thanks to my Dear Friend and fellow THUD NUT A.D. Smith for his special support in this and other projects.

John and I also wish to give a SPECIAL THANKS to our parents and family.

F.D. and Ruth Campbell.
Sedgefield and Wilda Hill
Linda, Jason and Jennifer Hill.

Without their love and support we would never be able to undertake and complete a project such as this.

Book Design by Ian Robertson.

Copyright © 1996 by John M. Campbell & Michael Hill
Library of Congress Catalog Number: 96-67102

Printed in China.
ISBN: 0-7643-0062-8

We are interested in hearing from authors with book ideas on related topics.

Published by Schiffer Publishing Ltd.
77 Lower Valley Road
Atglen, PA 19310
Please write for a free catalog.
This book may be purchased from the publisher.
Please include $2.95 postage.
Try your bookstore first.

FOREWORD

Not too many fighter pilots from the 1950s and early 1960s era would have bet a plugged nickel that the F-105 would ever be of much interest to anyone other than those flying them. The thought that another heavyweight Republic Aircraft Corporation fighter, this one with very little wing and designed as a nuclear weapons delivery vehicle, could ever become a sentimental favorite of the worldwide aviation community was unheard of.

Conjecture around the bar in the club centered on how big and heavy it would be and what would be a suitable name for the successor to the straight wing F-84 Superhog. Votes were pretty well split between Ultrahog and Lead Sled. It was almost a given that it would come with a dirt sniffer on the nose wheel, which was a standard Republic device that would not allow the aircraft to become airborne until it could smell the dirt off the far end of the runway. The concern was justified, since nobody knew anybody who had strapped on any model of the F-84 and been able to avoid high speed, gut-wrenching duels with the last few feet of concrete runway while trying to get airborne in the world's fastest tricycle.

Even the concept phase of the F-105 development was stormy and confused, as government and industry planners struggled to define what was needed in the way of a nuclear capable fighter. At the time the initial contracts were signed, about the only true agreement was that the first wing of the new machines was supposed to be combat ready by 1955. That schedule was in trouble from day one.

Historically, the rapport between the civilian aircraft contractors and their military customers had been great. The customer would tell all interested contractors what they wanted in the way of mission performance, speed, maintainability in a new aircraft. The contractors would respond with specific proposals, or flying prototypes, and after appropriate evaluation or competition, the customer would select a contractor and award a contract. The winning contractor, run by and staffed with experienced aviators, would build the machine, test it, provide the appropriate spare parts and maintenance instructions-then invite the involved military service to come to the factory to learn how to take over what they had purchased. It was fun to be involved with a new aircraft.

Company presidents and their top engineers often shared brown bag lunches with their workers while listening to new ideas along the production line, or while hangar flying with their pilots on the flight test ramp. But there were no brown bags when a fighter pilot visited to brief on military requirements or to be briefed on factory progress on the new machine. The visitor was greeted warmly, toured through the facility like royalty, and could count on at least a sumptuous two hour lunch in a plush spot, complete with lots of war stories. The system worked great and was highly honorable.

The Thud was cursed by the first serious new look at aircraft procurement, as Washington discovered cost effectiveness. The Secretary of Defense directed that the services change their basic ways of doing business with the contractors, which forced the contractors to change as well.

The military created new organizations to supervise the contractors, and the transition was seldom graceful, and often arrogant. Leadership criteria on both sides of the equation changed from seasoned aviators to non-pilots, qualified as Masters of Business Administration or the like, and harmony often became conflict. Having played this new game from both sides, I consider it a loser. There are no more brown bag lunches shared along the flightline these days, and that is a shame.

With hindsight, we can say that the F-105 was destined for success by virtue of making it through all that hassle and taking shape as the YF-105 prototype. But she was far from capable of fighting a war by 1955, in fact, 1955 was when the very first YF-105 rolled onto the dry lake bed of the flight test center at Edwards Air Force Base in California. Promises were that it would go supersonic on the first test flight, but if it happened, it could only have happened with the afterburner blazing while heading straight down for the desert floor. She fell far short of most of her performance expectations, and the Air Force had already decided that major redesign was going to be necessary, before a hung landing gear caused a crash landing and cut the program short at twenty two hours.

Nevertheless, one giant milestone had been passed. When this huge fighter touched down on landing, she was prone to do so with a resounding thud-and the nickname Thud, not necessarily given as a term of flattery, was on its way into aviation history.

So, it was back to the drawing board, along with 5,000 hours of National Aeronautics and Space Administration wind tunnel testing for both the F-105 and the F-102, neither one of which could get up to speed. The resulting coke bottle airframe concept that emerged from the NASA project proved highly successful for both aircraft, and was immediately incorporated into the early production F-105B model aircraft.

Conflict mounted again with the emergence of the F-105B, with some claiming program success, and others recommending cancellation of the entire F-105 program. The B model flew well, but it took 150 hours of ground maintenance time to generate one hour of flying time. There were practically no spare parts, for which the Air Force blamed the contractor while the contractor blamed the Air Force. Some thought the experimental North American YF-107 might be a better bet, but others demanded consideration of all the time, money, and effort that had already gone into the F-105. When the Thunderbirds wound up with a structurally damaged B model that shed a wing and killed Gene Devlin on their first show trip with F-105s, it looked to many like the Thud had reached the end of the road.

But, champ that she was, she hung in there. Despite the confusion caused by almost constant program changes, that saw contracts signed, canceled, and resigned, real design and equipment improvements went into the aircraft. By the time the D models, which represented the true production configuration, became available to the tactical units, she was a pretty reasonable machine, but was still plagued with maintenance and supply woes. It is a tribute to those who operated and supported the Thud through some very tough early times that by April of 1963, Tactical Air Command was able to accomplish an initial wing deployment of D models to Spain. The Thud began to slip into the worldwide readiness and deployment business.

The only reason for conducting Thud deployments, with long over water legs and constant refuelings, was to be ready to drop a nuke weapon anywhere in the world should that be required. The bird was designed for that mission, and had an internal bay for nuclear stores and cockpit systems to allow the pilot to get the nuclear job done. The mission was demanding of men and machines, and preparing for and practicing nuclear delivery techniques required full attention and all the flying hours that could be generated. Perseverance paid off, and the Thud and her crews reached a plateau when they were certified as competent and qualified nuclear weapons carriers.

Little or no time, effort, or thought was spent on conventional weapons or on the tactics and lessons learned from World War II and Korea. The smart people who were supposed to know were outspoken in their proclamations that machine guns and cannon were outmoded, that dumb iron bombs were simply historical leftovers, and that air-to-air combat as we had known it was a thing of the past. Then things got all wrapped around the axle in the Gulf of Tonkin, and the Thud and her pilots, who had finally earned some degree of mission respectability as nuclear capable fighters, were faced with the immediate challenge of fighting a conventional weapons war.

How does a nuke fighter enter a conventional war? Rather awkwardly at first, but with experienced and dedicated people and a solid Republic airframe, we got the job done rather quickly. The bomb bay became a fuel tank, the cannon in the nose became important again, and the care, handling, and loading of iron bombs all over the underside of the aircraft was of prime concern. Nuclear weapons cockpit systems became excess baggage, and time and distance and dead reckoning along a pencil line drawn on an unreliable map became the name of the game. Miles of lead and sight pictures and gunsight depression for high angle dive bombing were back in vogue.

We all knew we needed tanker support for long over water hauls, but when we got to Southeast Asia we quickly found out that we could not fight the war we were tasked to fight without tanker support. With all the burner we needed to get a max load Thud into the air from a jungle strip, we had to hit the tankers right after takeoff if we expected to be able to even get to the targets. Once you got into Pack Six and got back out, usually staring at a fuel needle approaching the bottom of the gauge and sometimes with holes all over that were spewing board chemicals into the atmosphere, it was either catch a tanker or step out over nasty territory. The tankers were officially restricted to refueling tracks designed to keep them well south of trouble. But when Thud drivers were coming out hurting, plenty of the good tanker guys ignored the rules and came after us, and they saved many a Thud driver.

Some of the newer Thud jocks had some rude experiences catching up on conventional weapons tactics that they had been denied the opportunity of learning properly, but there were plenty of old heads around to help. By the time the Rolling Thunder campaign gave us some access to Route Package Six and downtown Hanoi, the Thuds and the Thud drivers were ready and hungry. We carried seventy-five percent of the load up there and we did amazingly good and accurate work in the face of awesome defenses that were augmented by our own silly and often fatal restrictions on where we could go and how we could fight.

The electronic excellence of the Russian and Chinese supplied and directed air defenses and surface to air missile networks forced more changes, in a hurry. Our supporters broke all the records developing electronic counter measure pods for individual aircraft and condensing the development of the initial two place, anti-SAM Wild Weasels into a ridiculously short time frame. It was on-the-job training with real bullets, but it sure worked well. Who could think of fighting a war today without Wild Weasels?

We lost a lot of aircraft and a lot of good people because cost effectiveness, plus the original design requirements for the Thud had combined to cut the corners on protecting vital aircraft functions, such as fuel and hydraulic systems, from the golden beebee. Believe me, when even the villagers were laying on the ground, shooting muskets straight up, there were more than enough golden beebees flying around. We did get some helpful survival modifications as the war went on, but the amazing thing is that the Thud did such a great job fighting a war it was not designed for. It hauled huge loads through shocking weather, put the bombs right in the pickle barrel, out-dueled the MiGs, whipped the SAMS, survived some incredible battle damage, and got a lot of us back home. It is no wonder that those of us who had the opportunity to fly and fight up north thought of the Thud with affection. It is gratifying that now, long after her fighting days, the entire aviation community embraces the legend of the Thud.

Fighter aircraft do have personalities, at least to those who fly them, and they do have pedigrees, at least to those who investigate the detail. Ask a Thud driver about his aircraft and he will give you the last three tail numbers and tell you it was a good, bad, or indifferent machine. Ask a Thud aficionado about the same Thud and he can probably tell you the full serial number, when it first rolled onto the flightline, and on and on. It takes both to tell the story, and I personally thank Mike Hill and John Campbell for the thorough and demanding research job they have done in putting Role Call: Thud together.

Just perusing some sections of the draft brought back memories of Thud personalities for me. The first thing I looked for was my bird, 338, which I named Alice's Joy, and I immediately thought of Sergeant Willis and all the others who kept her in one piece. Actually, after we had been fighting for awhile, most of them were pasted together parts and pieces of each other. I remembered that when I last strapped 338 on for my next to last mission over there on June 11, 1967, I had somebody else's canopy on her, replacing the one that I had managed to get shot up a few days before. That afternoon she brought me back from one of the wildest rides I ever had, with a huge hole in the vertical fin, and the fin barely hanging onto the rear fuselage. Good bird.

The next morning I flew 450, while my guys were scrounging a vertical fin to paste 338 back together. I really got tagged on that last one, and the rear end of 450 burned for twenty minutes coming out of Hanoi before I could nurse her up high enough so that the lack of oxygen put the fire out. She got me back as far as Udorn, and the last I saw of that tough machine, she was being tugged towards the junk yard. I don't know how, or with which parts of other aircraft, but I found out from "Roll Call: Thud" that she came back to fight again.

On July 13th my friend Carl Osborne took the latest version of 450 to Route Pack One, where he got clobbered, but made it across the Thai border. Ozzie punched out and was rescued, but 450 augered. Three three eight made it until September 2nd, when she was shot down in Route Pack One and Major William Bennett was killed in action. Thanks for the info Mike and John. I would never have had those pieces of personal history without your efforts. I am sure that many will share my appreciation of your fine work.

Colonel Jack Broughton
USAF(Retired)

Left: Colonel Jack Broughton and **Alice's Joy** bring each other back from another trip to "Downtown Hanoi."

INTRODUCTION

She was designed and built with one purpose in mind. She was to be Tactical Air Command's primary nuclear fighter bomber. Built by Republic at "the foundry", this large hulk of aluminum was given the designation F-105.

All newly designed aircraft undergo growing pains. In the case of the F-105 the pains and problems were almost terminal. There were so many of them that the Air Force kept starting and stopping the program until it seemed nobody really knew what was going on with the new airplane. One after another the problems were fixed until the rough outline of the big 105 was as sturdy as man could make it.

The pilots who had flown the 105 were impressed with her. She was big, roomy and built like the well-known brick outhouse. Once she got into the air she was a good piece of airplane to fly. She would go like a bat out of hell down low on the deck. Most pilots believed that all you had to do was trim her out, point her nose in the right direction and she would fly just about anywhere.

All new aircraft need an official name. Republic Aviation had always called their aircraft Thunder-something. To go along with Thunderbolt, Thunderjet and Thunderstreak, Republic called the 105 Thunderchief. Likewise, most aircraft acquire an unofficial nickname somewhere along their service life.

There are several stories as to how the 105 was tagged with her nickname. One was based on the resounding sound she made if she contacted the ground or runway rather hard. Another story was based on a character on the Howdy Doody Show. An Indian chief, complete with feathered war bonnet, was known as Chief ThunderThud. Since the 105 was the ThunderChief, the nickname ThunderThud was a logical choice.

No matter how it came about, the name THUD attached itself to the F-105. At first it was a disdainful slur on the fine new machine. As time went on and the F-105 proved herself the fine machine she was, it became one of the most honored names in aviation history.

Thankfully, the THUD was never called upon to fulfill the mission she was designed for. Regrettably, she was called on to fight a war for which she was not designed at all. She went from a tactical nuclear bomber to a strategic iron bomber. It seems that in all her political wisdom at the time, the United States became embroiled in a feeble attempt to keep dominos from falling in Southeast Asia.

It was supposed to be a limited war. As such it had limited, if any, clear cut goals set forth to win. It seemed that the only real goal was to restrict the conduct of the war to the point where there could be no hope of winning. Secretary of Defense Robert McNamara had stated that according to all the information he had, there was no way that the war could be won. With that he set about to fulfill his statements with self defeating policies. Final control rested with President Lyndon Johnson, who didn't want an outhouse bombed unless he said it was alright. With command and control like that resting thousands of miles from where the real action was, the THUD Drivers didn't need anymore enemies.

Day after day the THUD Drivers were "fragged" for various targets. They would strap into their planes and hurl themselves at the heaviest air defenses in the history of aerial warfare. They completed their missions in the tradition of the Air Force, regardless of the criminal restrictions placed on them by the government they had sworn to defend and uphold.

As the war moved on, halted, and then opened up repeatedly, the THUD losses mounted. Some pilots were killed, and others would suffer inhumane treatment in the hell hole that was known as the Hanoi Hilton. No matter what was thrown at them, be it MiGs, AAA, or SAMs, the THUD Drivers lived up to the catch phrase, "Press On Regardless". The men who flew and the men who kept the THUD flying wrote a new chapter in the history of the Air Force. It is hopeful that someday they will be able to take their rightful place as heroes in our country's history books.

This book is not a technical history of the THUD. That has been done before. Nor are we attempting an all encompassing history of the THUD and the units that flew her. We will let someone else write about the technical subsystems and specifications of this grand old bird.

Our purpose is to pay tribute to the THUD, her drivers, and the men who kept her flying. What better way to perpetuate that memory, then in photographs of as many different serial numbers as possible.

Regrettably, we could not find a photo of all 833 THUDS that were built. Rest assured some of them were never photographed. Some of the photos we needed rest in collections, boxes or albums across the country. In spite of this we have been able to present over 60% of the aircraft that were built. John and I believe that this is significant in that there have never been as many photos of THUDs in one book before.

We have tried to obtain the best photos possible to use in this book. In some cases we have used photos that are not the sharpest or best color. We used these photos in cases where it was the only photo of a serial number that was available to us. With this in mind your special THUD just might be represented within these pages.

In cases where we do not have a photo we have included the production number, serial number and a caption telling what we know about the aircraft. Thus, even though we don't have a photo, we present the information just in case your THUD was not photographed.

John and I hope that you will find your special THUD within these pages. We hope that this work will stand as a fitting tribute to the thousands of men who were associated with the THUD at one time or another. With that in mind, "Clean em up, Green em up, Start your music," and enjoy our ROLE CALL: THUD.

John M. Campbell
Michael D. Hill

1 ▲

2▲

1   54-0098   YF-105A
First of the line. This prototype was delivered and flown for the first time in October 1955. She crash landed at Edwards AFB December 16, 1955. (USAF)

2   54-0099   YF-105A
Second THUD built. She was used as a test aircraft for the program. Shown here testing the buddy refueling system. (USAF)

3   54-0100   YF-105B
Designated as a YF-105B, she was the third airframe built. She was used as a test aircraft. Photo taken at Edwards Air Force Base in May 1958. (Campbell Archives /OKC)

4   54-0101   YF-105B
The second YF-105B built also served as a test aircraft until crashing at Eglin Air Force Base in May 1958. (Swendrowski)

5   54-0102   YF-105B
Her service life was spent as a test aircraft. Retired on May 21, 1960, she now resides in a place of honor at the U.S.S. Alabama Memorial Park, Mobile Alabama. (USAF)

3 ▲

4 ▼

5 ▼

6▲

7▲

8▲

6   54-0103   YF-105B
Her service life started on March 5, 1958, and continued as a test ship at Edwards until she retired. Her last duty was with the Navy at their Explosive Ordence Disposal facility.

7   54-0104   F-105B
The seventh airframe built by Republic. She was the first true B model of the F-105. Used as a ground training aircraft at Chanute AFB.
(Minert Collection)

8   54-0106   F-105B
On December 15, 1969, she crashed into the Atlantic Ocean, killing Republic test pilot Martin Signorelli during acceptance flight. (Satterfield)

9   54-0107   F-105B
The third F-105B built, she was used for Phase 5 testing.

10   54-0109   F-105B
Assigned to the F-105 test program, she served most of her service life at Eglin AFB. Retired to Amarillo AFB.

9 ▼

10 ▼

11▲   12▲

11   54-0110   F-105B
Written off at Brookley AFB, September 30, 1960. (Republic)

12   54-0111   F-105B
She was the first F-105 airframe to reach an operational unit. Written off January 23, 1961, at Brookley AFB. (USAF)

13   54-0105   JF-105
Designated as the first JF-105 which was to be the photo version of the F-105. She is preserved at Lackland AFB. (Miller)

14   54-0108   JF-105
Designated as second JF-105 photo recon version, she served as a test aircraft until written off November 20, 1959. (Republic)

14 ▼   13▲

15▲

15   54-0112   JF-105
The third JF-105 spent its service life as JF-105 a test aircraft. Scrapped October 1975. (Moffitt)

16   57-5776   F-105B
The first production aircraft to reach an Air Force unit. Preserved at McGuire AFB, New Jersey. (Minert Collection)

17   57-5777   F-105B
Crashed into Long Island Sound during a test flight October 11, 1958.

18   57-5778   F-105B
Photographed in September 1974 while serving with the New Jersey Air National Guard. (Spering)

19   57-5779   F-105B
First assigned to the 335th TFS in 1958. Shown here serving with the New Jersey Air National Guard in August 1975. (Spering)

16▲

18▼

19▼

▲20   22▲

20   57-5780   F-105B
Photographed in the colors of the New Jersey National Guard. (Stewart)

21   57-5781   F-105B
Crashed on December 2, 1960, in Belport Bay, Long Island, NY, due to engine fire. Capt. Ray Kingston ejected.

22   57-5782   F-105B
Originally assigned to the 335th TFS. One of nine F-105B's to be assigned to the USAF Aerobatics Team, the Thunderbirds.

23   57-5783   F-105B
Photographed while serving with the New Jersey Air Guard. She is preserved at the Cradle of Aviation Museum.

24   57-5784   F-105B
Photographed July 29, 1979, serving with the New Jersey Air National Guard. She was preserved at the Pima Air Museum for awhile. Current location unknown, possibly Mexico.

23▲   ▲24

25▲

26▲

27▲

25 57-5785 F-105B
Crashed February 27, 1963, at Avon Park Range, Florida. (Strnad)

26 57-5786 F-105B
Crashed July 18, 1963, near Jonesville, SC. (Strnad)

27 57-5787 F-105B
One of nine F-105B's assigned to the Air Force Thunderbirds, she finished her service life with the New Jersey Air National Guard. (Spering)

28 57-5788 F-105B
Photographed in May 1970 while serving with the New Jersey Air National Guard. Crashed January 16, 1970, killing Major William Dimas. (Soldeus)

29 57-5789 F-105B
Her last unit was the 141th TFS New Jersey ANG. This example of the F-105B is preserved at Brookes AFB, Texas. (Spering)

28▼

29▼

30 ▲

30   57-5790   F-105B
Follows a brother THUNDERBIRD back to the parking ramp. She caught fire after take off February 2, 1971. She crashed near McGuire AFB. (Minert Collection)

31   57-5791   F-105B
Crashed April 7, 1980, while serving with the New Jersey Air National Guard. (Spering)

32   57-5792   F-105B
Wearing the colors of the 141st TFS, New Jersey Air National Guard, this example was photographed in August 1975. (Spering)

33   57-5793   F-105B
From the New Jersey Air National Guard, August 1975. She was one of nine F-105B's that served with the USAF Thunderbirds. She is preserved at the Air Force Museum. (Spering)

32▼

31▲   **33▼**

34 ▲

35 ▲

34   57-5794   F-105B
Crashed on March 18, 1960, near Eglin AFB, FL. (Strnad)

35   57-5795   F-105B
Assigned to the New Jersey Air National Guard, this photo was taken at Edwards AFB in February 1976. (Rotramel)

36   57-5796   F-105B
Armed with two Sidewinder missiles, this New Jersey Air National Guard F-105B was photographed in May 1970. Crashed August 4, 1971, near NAS Lakehurst killing Lt. John W. Anderson. (Spering)

37   57-5797   F-105B
One of nine F-105B's assigned to the USAF Thunderbirds. She finished her career with the New Jersey Air Guard. Photo taken May 23, 1971. (Spering)

38   57-5798   F-105B
She finished her flying days with the New Jersey Air Guard . She was one of nine aircraft assigned to the USAF Thunderbird Aerobatics Team. Crashed June 27, 1975, at Luke AFB. (Soldeus)

39   57-5799   F-105B
Suffered an explosion during engine cartridge start at Eglin AFB, August 29, 1959.

36 ▲

37 ▼

38 ▼

40▲

41▲

40   57-5800   F-105B
Crashed June 12, 1961, due to compressor failure.

41   57-5801   F-105B Crashed May 9, 1964, due to structure failure during pitch up for landing during Thunderbird arrival at Hamilton AFB, California. Major Gene Devlin was fatally injured in the crash. (Republic/Robert D. Archer)

42   57-5802   F-105B
Photographed at McGuire AFB, New Jersey, this F-105B is one of the nine assigned to the USAF Thunderbirds. Lost due to in flight fire caused by the Vulcan cannon jamming October 4, 1976. (Mayer)

43   57-5803   F-105B
Photographed in June 1974 while serving with the 466th TFS at Hill AFB, Utah. This THUD was retired to March AFB, where she is preserved.

44   57-5804   SF-105B
Shown in the markings of the New Jersey Air National Guard in August 1974. (Spering)

42▲

43▼

44▼

45▲

47▲

45 57-5805   F-105B
Crashed June 28, 1960, in Pamlico Bay, NC. (Strnad)

46 57-5806   F-105B
Crashed August 20, 1965, near Pahrump, Nevada, due to engine problem. (Strnad)

47 57-5807   F-105B
Originally assigned to the 334th TFS at Seymour Johnson AFB. Crashed June 7, 1963. (USAF)

48 57-5808   F-105B
She finished her service life with the 466th TFS at Hill AFB. Photographed September 10, 1974. (Miller)

49 57-5809   F-105B
Crashed November 14, 1961, near Seymour Johnson AFB, NC.

50 57-5810   F-105B
Shown taking off from the Republic factory. She crashed July 29, 1960, near Florence, AZ. (USAF)

51 57-5811   F-105B
Photographed in October 1969 while serving with the New Jersey Air National Guard. Crashed near Seymour Johnson AFB September 26, 1977. (Soldeus)

48▲

50▼

51▼

52 ▲

53 ▲

52   57-5812   F-105B
Serving with the 466th TFS on a snow covered ramp at Hill AFB in January 1974. (Knowles)

53   57-5813   F-105B
Photographed in the markings of the 466th TFS at Hill AFB, Utah in January 1974. Scrapped at Kelly AFB, TX.

54   57-5814   F-105B
She served as Thunderbird 1 while flying with the team. Shown here with the 466th TFS at Hill AFB, Utah, in January 1974, she is preserved at Salt Lake City. (Knowles)

55   57-5815   F-105B
Her first unit was the 334th TFS at Seymour Johnson AFB. She finished her flying career with the New Jersey Air National Guard. (Spering)

56   57-5816   F-105B
Shown in the marking of the 466th TFS, 508th TFG on June 11, 1973, at Hill AFB, Utah. (Minert Collection)

54 ▲

▼55

56▲

57 57-5817 F-105B
First assigned to 334th TFS at Seymour Johnson AFB. Shown here in the markings of the 466th TFS at Hill AFB, June 1977. (Minert)

58 57-5818 F-105B
(Center) Crashed September 30, 1960, near Mauk, GA. (USAF)

59 57-5819 F-105B
Photographed in August 1974 while serving with the 466th TFS at Hill AFB, Utah.

57▲
58▼

59▼

▲ 62   60 ▲

60   57-5820   F-105B
Serving with the 466th TFS, 310th TFW at Hill AFB, Utah, in June 1977. Preserved at the Florida Military Aviation Museum, Clearwater. (Geer)

61   57-5821   F-105B
Refueling from a tanker in June 1961 while serving with the 4th TFW. This F-105B crashed on March 16, 1962. The crash occurred at Nellis AFB. (Alexander)

62   57-5822   F-105B
Crashed November 18, 1962, 1.5 miles east of McCoy AFB. (Strnad)

63   57-5823   F-105B
Shown in the markings for the 466th TFS, 508th TFG at Hill AFB, Utah, January 23, 1974. Preserved at Fairchild AFB. (Knowles)

64   57-5824   F-105B
Crashed April 16, 1963, while landing at Seymour Johnson AFB due to loss of control while landing.

61 ▲   ▼ 63

66 ▲

69▲

70▼

68▲

65   57-5825   F-105B
Crashed September 21, 1961, Indian Springs, Nevada, due to control malfunction.

66   57-5826   F-105B
As she appeared in August 1973 while serving her final days with the 466th TFS at Hill AFB. (Loomis)

67   57-5827   F-105B
Crashed October 27, 1961, at Seymour Johnson AFB, NC.

68   57-5828   F-105B
Crashed February 28, 1963, near LaGrange, NC. Pilot ejected at 8000 ft. (Strnad)

69   57-5829   F-105B
Photographed November 5, 1966 while serving with the 141st TFS, New Jersey Air National Guard. (Morris)

70   57-5830   F-105B
She wears the markings of the 141st TFS, New Jersey Air National Guard, in August 1975. Crashed near McGuire AFB, February 5, 1980. (Spering)

71   57-5831   F-105B
She finished her active service with the 466th TFS at Hill AFB, Utah. Photographed on September 10, 1974. Crashed March 3, 1979. (Miller)

71▼

73 ▲

72   57-5832   F-105B
Crashed June 17, 1961, after flame-out at Eglin Aux. Field 2, FL.

73   57-5833   F-105B
After serving with the 466th TFS at Hill AFB, she was transferred to Tinker AFB, Oklahoma City, Oklahoma, to serve as a battle damage repair trainer. (Dienst)

74   57-5834   F-105B
She wears the markings of the 466th TFS. That was the last active duty she served in before crashing on October 6, 1980. (Minert Collection)

75   57-5835   F-105B
Shown in the markings for the 23rd TFG, better known as "The Flying Tigers", she was visiting Richards-Gebour AFB, on September 14, 1969. (Minert Collection)

74 ▲

75▲

76▲

76   57-5836   F-105B
Photographed in the markings of the New Jersey Air National Guard, this aircraft crashed into Chesapeake Bay on March 3, 1974.

77   57-5837   F-105B
Served with the New Jersey Air National Guard. She is preserved at Castle AFB, California. (Miller)

78   57-5838   F-105B
Serving with the 4519th CCTS, 23rd TFW at McConnell AFB, Kansas, in September, 1968. (Robinson)

79   57-5839   F-105B
Serving with the New Jersey Air National Guard on July 5, 1972. She is preserved at Ellsworth AFB, South Dakota. (Kuhn)

77▲

78▲

79▼

80 ▲

80   57-5840   F-105B
The last F-105B built. She is shown
here after an emergency landing at Hill
AFB, Utah, in 1974. (Minert Collection)

81   58-1146   F-105D
The first F-105D built, first flight June
9, F-105D 1959. Crashed at Farmingdale, N.Y, September 26, 1960. (Campbell Archives /OKC)

82   58-1147   F-105D
Written off and salvaged March 26,
1968, at McClellan AFB.

83   58-1148   F-105D
Crashed March 17, 1962, at Eglin AFB.

84   58-1149   F-105D
Crashed June 15, 1965, near Eglin
AFB while serving as a test aircraft.
(Strnad)

81 ▲

84 ▼

85▲

86▲

87▲

88▼

85   58-1150   F-105D
Crashed June 26, 1968, while serving with the 34th TFS at Korat Thailand. Nicknamed **THE BOSS/COBRA** while serving with 34th TFS. Photographed at Nellis AFB in 1961. (Robert D. Archer)

86   58-1151   F-105D
Shot down by a MiG-21, April 28, 1967, over RP5/NVN. Captain F.A. Caras listed as MIA.

87   58-1152   F-105D
Serving with the 44TFS at Korat. She carried the nicknames **THE REBEL, MISS MARY, ARKANSAS RAZOR-BACK, DAS JAEGER, REPUBLIC'S EDSEL,** and **THE RIPPER.** She crashed near McConnell AFB, June 16, 1971, due to engine failure.

88   58-1153   F-105D
Shot down by groundfire over RP6A/NVN on April 26, 1967. Captain W.M. Meyer KIA.

▲ 89

90▲

92 ▲

89   58-1154   F-105D
Shot down over RP6B/NVN by 85mm gunfire. Captain Wallace Newcomb ejected to become a POW. (Strnad)

90   58-1155   F-105D
The tenth D airframe built, thus she was known as D-10 while serving as a test aircraft. Her last unit was 121st TFS, D.C. Air National Guard, where she was photographed on July 11, 1975.

91   58-1156   F-105D
Hit by groundfire over RP6, she crashed into the sea on January 21, 1967. Captain W.R. Wyatt was rescued. Credited with a MiG 17 kill June 26, 1966.

92   58-1157   F-105D
Known as **SHIRLEY ANN** and **BUBBLES**, she was shot down by a MiG-21 over RP6A, NVN on January 3, 1968. Colonel James Bean ejected to become a POW.

93   58-1158   F-105D
Photographed while serving with the 4th TFW. Crashed April 15, 1966, due to engine problems, while assigned to the 469th TFS at Korat. (Via Robert D. Archer)

94   58-1159   F-105D
Wearing the colors of the D.C Air National Guard, she was photographed at Andrews AFB, July 11, 1975. (Minert Collection)

93▲   ▼ 94

95 58-1160 F-105D
Crashed December 10, 1966, while serving with the 357th TFS at Takhli due to engine failure.

96 58-1161 F-105D
Crashed at Korat, Thailand, November 22, 1966, due to engine failure. (Campbell Archive/OKC)

97 58-1162 F-105D
Crashed October 1, 1964, at McConnell AFB.

98 58-1163 F-105D
Shot down over RP6, NVN on July 29, 1967. Lt. J. Benton West rescued. (See 58-1161)

99 58-1164 F-105D
Shot down May 22, 1966 by AAA over Laos. Pilot R.A. Hackford rescued. (See 58-1161)

100 58-1165 F-105D
Lost to AA fire over RP1, July 17, 1966. Lt. W.C Spelius rescued.

101 58-1166 F-105D
Crashed April 16, 1962, due to structural failure during LABS Pull-up. Captain Charles Lamb, Jr., was killed.

102 58-1167 F-105D
Nicknamed **MISS UNIVERSE** and **MARY B.** She flew three hundred miles back to her base after having her right elevator shot away by ground fire. Scrapped at McClellan AFB May 1, 1973.

96▲

102▼

▲104

103   58-1168   F-105D
Known as **BETTY'S BOY**, she was lost to groundfire on October 25, 1967, near the Paul Doumer Bridge, NVN. Major Richard Smith ejected to become a POW. Credited with a MiG 17 kill April 19, 1967. (USAF).

104   58-1169   F-105D
She carried the nickname **DRAGON**. Shot down October 5, 1967, by AAA. Major Konrad Trautman POW. (Larsen)

105   58-1170   F-105D
Lost November 19, 1967, to a SAM over RP6, NVN. Major Raymond Vissotzky, POW. Photographed at Edwards AFB, 1961. (Robert D. Archer)

106   58-1171   F-105D
Hit by groundfire over RP1 and crashed at sea June 3, 1966. Captain R.D. Pielin rescued.

107   58-1172   F-105D
She was known as **DAISEY MAE-STUD THUD** with the 13th TFS. Crashed in September 1976. (Minert Collection)

105▼   103▲

▼107

108▲

110▲

111▲

113▲

108 58-1173   F-105D
Shown with sixteen 750 pound bombs. The heaviest bomb load carried by a single engine fighter. (Minert Collection)

109 59-1717   F-105D
Crashed due to engine failure January 20, 1967, at Takhli while serving with the 333rd TFS.

110 59-1718   F-105D
Photographed at Edwards AFB, May 1963. Lost to groundfire over RP4 NVN, May 7, 1965. Major R.E. Lambert rescued. (Robert D. Archer)

111 59-1719   F-105D
Shown in the 4th TFW markings, she was lost to ground fire over Laos on January 16, 1966. Captain D.C. Wood listed as MIA. (Minert Collection)

112 59-1720   F-105D
Shot down August 21, 1967, by AAA over RP6, while serving with the 333TFS. Captain M.L. Morrill MIA.

113 59-1721   F-105D
Shot down by AAA over RP1 on June 22, 1966. Captain J.D. Whipple rescued.

114 59-1722   F-105D
Hit by groundfire over RP1 July 1, 1966. Captain Lewis Shattuck ejected and was rescued.

115 59-1723   F-105D
Shown in her early natural metal finish. Shot down May 27, 1967, by a SAM over RP6A/NVN. Captain Gordon Blackwood listed as MIA. (Geer/Campbell Archives /OKC)

▼115

▲121

116 59-1724 F-105D
Lost in a mid-air accident with a O-1 Birddog aircraft while serving with the 355TFW at Takhli on March 2, 1966.

117 59-1725 F-105D
Lost December 8, 1966, over RP6/NVN. Lt. Col. Don H. Asire, commander of the 354TFS, listed as KIA.

118 59-1726 F-105D
Shot down by a MiG 17 on a mission to Hanoi, April 30, 1967. Lt. Robert Abbott ejected to become a POW.

119 59-1727 F-105D
Lost October 3, 1967. Hit by a SAM during a mission to Dap Cau Bypass RR Bridge. Major Robert Barnett ejected to become a POW.

123▼

120 59-1728 F-105D
Hit by groundfire over RP6 on May 12, 1967. Captain Earl Grenzebach listed as MIA.

121 59-1729 F-105D
Known as **TAKHLI TAXI** and **ANDY CAPP**, she was credited with a SAM site kill. She crashed on July 14, 1978, while serving at Tinker AFB, Oklahoma. (Soldeus)

122 59-1730 F-105D
Crashed January 11, 1961, near Eglin AFB, FL.

123 59-1731 F-105D
Photographed at Byrd Field, Virginia, in the colors of the Virginia Air National Guard on May 3, 1980. During her com-bat in Southeast Asia she carried the name **FRITO BANDITO**. While serving in the Air National Guard she was known as **THE HUN'S HAMMER.** (Miller)

▲ 124

125
◀

129
◀

124   59-1732   F-105D
Serving with the District of Columbia Air National Guard on May 25, 1979. (Miller)

125   59-1733   F-105D
Last served with the 121st TFS at Andrews AFB. Retired to AMARC. (Strnad)

126   59-1734   F-105D
Lost November 4, 1969, to groundfire over Laos. Captain L.J. Hanley is listed as MIA.

127   59-1735   F-105D
Shot down by AAA during a mission to Phuc Yen Airfield October 25, 1967. Captain Ramon Horinek became a POW.

128   59-1736   F-105D
Shot down over Laos on January 11, 1966, while serving with the 334TFS at Takhli. Captain J.R. Stell was rescued.

129   59-1737   F-105D
Known as **CHERRY BOY** while serving with the 469th TFS. She crashed at Tan Son Nhut after collision with a C-123. (Larson)

130 59-1738   F-105D   ▲130   ▲131
Serving with the DC Air National Guard
on July 11, 1975, She is preserved at
Dyess AFB, Texas. (KAHS)

131 59-1739   F-105D
During her career she carried several
names. To the 34th TFS she was
known as **RUM RUNNER** while the
354th called her **BULLDOG 1.** During
service with the Virginia Air National
Guard she was called **QUEEN OF THE
FLEET**. (Bailey)

132 59-1740   F-105D
Crashed June 19, 1962, near Indian
Springs, Nevada. (Strnad)

133 59-1741   F-105D
Lost to AAA over RP5 on July 7, 1966.
Captain Jack Tomes ejected and was
captured.

134 59-1742   F-105D
Shot down April 5, 1965, by AAA over
RP3. Captain T. Gay ejected and was
rescued. (USAF)

135 59-1743   F-105D
Shown as **HANOI EXPRESS** serving
with the 149th TFS 192nd TFG on April
25, 1979. During her combat days she
was known as **LEAD ZEPPELIN, AR-
KANSAS TRAVELER, DARN DAGO.**
(Spering))

132▲

134▼   135▼

140▲

◄137

141▲

▼142

136 59-1744   F-105D
Crashed May 13, 1964, at Nellis AFB
due to loss of power on take off.

137 59-1745   F-105D
Lost to AAA over RP3 on March 31,
1967. Captain H.J. Henningar was
rescued.(USAF)

138 59-1746   F-105D
Lost to AAA over Laos on May 25,
1966. Lt. Hunter listed as KIA.

139 59-1747   F-105D
Crashed March 21, 1967, at Osan AFB.

140 59-1748   F-105D
Hit by AAA over RP6 on July 17, 1967.
Major H.C. Copeland ejected and was
taken POW. (USAF/Robert D. Archer)

141 59-1749   F-105D
MR.TOAD/MARILEE, 469TH TFS at
Korat. She was lost to AAA. Major D.S.
Aunapu ejected and was rescued.
(Larsen)

142 59-1750   F-105D
THE FLYING ANVIL IV from the 469th
TFS at Korat. She was lost to AAA over
RP6 on December 14, 1967. Captain
James Sehorn was taken POW.
(Larson)

143 59-1751   F-105D
Crashed February 27, 1964.

144 59-1752   F-105D
Shot down by AAA on August 23, 1967,
during a mission to Bac Giang Bridge.
Major Elmo Baker ejected to become
a POW. Nicknamed **YANKEE SKY
DOG.**

145 59-1753   F-105D
Shot down May 18, 1965, over Laos.
Captain David Hrdlicka ejected but was
killed in action.

146 59-1754   F-105D
Shot down by a MiG 17 April 4, 1965,
during a mission to the Thanh Hoa
Bridge. Major Frank Bennett KIA.
(Strnad)

146▲

156▲

147 59-1755   F-105D
Shot down by a MiG 17 on July 19, 1966. Lt. S.W. Diamond is listed as MIA.

148 59-1756   F-105D
Crashed May 5, 1962, near Seymour Johnson AFB, NC. Captain C.R. Maddox was killed.

149 59-1757   F-105D
First assigned to the 4920th Combat Crew Training Wing at Nellis AFB. Crashed March 3, 1966. (See 59-1770)

150 59-1758   F-105D
Shot down over Laos on December 5, 1967. Major D.M. Russel KIA.

151 59-1759   F-105D
MISS CAROL/ SHORT PICTURE (MY DEE/ROSA) over North Vietnam November 1966. She was written off while serving with the District of Columbia Air National Guard on October 5, 1976. (Arruda/Isham)

152 59-1760   F-105D
Know as **LEMON SUCKER, WARLORD II, THE UNDERDOG** and **LADY JANE**. Crashed in April 1977 while serving with the District of Columbia Air National Guard.

153 59-1761   F-105D
Shot down by antiaircraft fire over RP6 on July 15, 1966. Captain C.L. Hamby ejected and was rescued.

154 59-1762   F-105D
Tucks up her gear for a mission with the 355th TFW at Takhli. Shot down September 12, 1968, over RP1. Major S.C. Maxwell listed as MIA. (Campbell Archives /OKC)

155 59-1763   F-105D
Lost to groundfire on August 14, 1966, over RP6 NVN. Captain Curtis Eaton listed as MIA.

151▲

▼154

157 ►

158 ▲

156 59-1764 F-105D
Lost to a MiG 17 April 4, 1965, on a mission to the Thanh Hoa Bridge. Captain James Magnusson Jr. listed as MIA.

157 59-1765 F-105D
Crashed at sea after being hit by groundfire on June 23, 1968. Major J.W. Aldep survived and was rescued. (Pepperill)

158 59-1766 F-105D
Shot down February 28, 1967, over RP1. Capt. J.S. Walbridge ejected and was picked up safely. (Minert Collection)

159 59-1767 F-105D
Crashed near McConnell AFB, June 28, 1967.

160 59-1768 F-105D
Crashed in Thailand after being hit over Laos by groundfire. Major W.E. Thurman was rescued. Photographed at Nellis AFB in June 1962. (Malerba)

161 59-1769 F-105D
Serving with the DC Air National Guard at Andrews Air Force Base. (Soldeus)

◄160

▼161

162▲

163▲

162   59-1770   F-105D
Shot down August 21, 1966. Captain Norman Wells was rescued. (USAF)

163   59-1771   F-105D
Serving with the Virginia Air National Guard September 5, 1979. During combat she carried the name **FOLEY'S FOLLY/OHIO EXPRESS.** Also known as **UNDERDOG II** and **DYNAMIC DUO**

164   59-1772   F-105D
Crashed in Laos after being hit by groundfire on January 20, 1970. Major D.W. Livingston was rescued. Credited with a MiG 17 kill on March 26, 1967, and another on April 29, 1967. (Meyerson)

165   59-1773   F-105D
Crashed May 23, 1963. (Soldeus)

164   165

166▲

168▼

166 59-1774   F-105D
Shown in the colors of the D.C. National Guard . She was retired to AMARC after her service life was over. (Minert Collection)

167 59-1817   F-105D
Collided with a Navion and crashed near Nellis AFB, April 1, 1963. Captain Edward Klostermav was killed.

168 59-1818   F-105D
Hit by AAA over Laos on August 25, 1969. Major S.R. Sanders KIA. (via Robert D. Archer)

169 59-1819   F-105D
Shot down May 10, 1966, over Laos by AAA. Lt. G.L. Clouser rescued. (See 59-1770)

170 59-1820   F-105D
Shot down December 2, 1966, over RP6/NVN killing Captain Marty Moorberg. He was awarded the Air Force Cross.

171 59-1821   F-105D
Crashed February 3, 1964.

172   59-1822   F-105D
THE POLISH GLIDER served with the 44th TFS during 1970 . Later she served with the Virginia Air National Guard as SUPERHOG. She was retired to AMARC. (Minert Collection)

173   59-1823   F-105D
Shot down by AAA over RP3 on December 21, 1965. Captain James Sullivan ejected and was rescued. (Steiger/Isham)

174   59-1824   F-105D
Crashed due to fuel stravation October 3, 1967, in Thailand.

175   59-1825   F-105D
Shot down over RP3 on March 15, 1967. Lt/Col. Peter Fredrick listed as MIA. (See 60-0411-2nd from top.)

176   59-1826   F-105D
Crashed at Homestead AFB, August 23, 1965.

177   60-0409   F-105D
THUNDER VALLEY from the 388th TFW. Crashed at sea after being hit by groundfire over RP1 May 31, 1968. Major E.P. Beresik was listed as KIA. Also known as BUNNY BABY. (USAF/ Robert D. Archer)

178   60-0410   F-105D
Crashed June 19, 1962, in Indian Springs, Nevada. (Green)

179   60-0411   F-105D
(Top) Lost to AAA over RP5/NVN, March 16, 1966. Major P.G. Underwood listed as MIA. (USAF)

180   60-0412   F-105D
Crashed May 14, 1964, near Wendover, Utah, due to inflight fire.

172▲

▼177

173▼

◄179 ▲178

181 60-0413   F-105D
Shot down over RP1 July 2, 1967. Major R.E. Stone Rescued.

182 60-0414   F-105D
Crashed August 13, 1969, while serving with the 23rd TFW at McConnell AFB, Kansas. (Green)

183 60-0415   F-105D
Lost to enemy AA fire over RP1. Major David Coons Rescued.

184 60-0416   F-105D
Crashed near McConnell AFB, Kansas, October 19, 1968.

182▼

▲185   ▲186

185 60-0417 F-105D
Lost to groundfire February 12, 1969.
Major V. Colasuonno Killed In Action.
(Plunkett)

186 60-0418 F-105D
Hit by SA/2 over RP6 February 14,
1968. Captain R.M. Elliot listed MIA.
She carried the name **SUGAR
BUGGER** while serving with the 388th
TFW. (USAF/Robert D. Archer)

187 60-0419 F-105D
Crashed October 30, 1963.

188 60-0420 F-105D
Crashed February 25, 1963, near Nellis
AFB, Nevada. (Green)

189 60-0421 F-105D
Known as **THE GREAT PUMPKIN**
while serving with the 469th TFS. She
was shot down May 14, 1967, by a SA/
2 over RP6. Major J.R. Wilson rescued.
(Larsen)

190 60-0422 F-105D
She carried the nickname **THE RED
BARON** with the 469th TFS. Shot
down December 17, 1967, by a MiG-
21 over RP6. Captain Jeffery Ellis
ejected to become a POW. (Larsen)

191 60-0423 F-105D
She carried the names **BUTTERFLY
BOMBER, SEXY SHEILA** with the
44th TFS at Korat. She was written off
December 11, 1967. (Minert Collection)

188 ▲

▼189   ▼190

191▲

192 ▲

194 ▲

192 60-0424   F-105D
Known as **MICKEY TITTY CHI** with the 34th TFS. Hit by flak over RP5, crashing in Laos, July 10, 1967. Major M.E. Seavers Jr. rescued. (Larson)

193 60-0425   F-105D
Lost October 17, 1967, over RP6. Major Dwight Sullivan listed as a POW.

194 60-0426   F-105D
Shot down April 2, 1967, over RP1. Captain John Dramesi ejected and was taken prisoner.

195 60-0427   F-105D
Crashed at Korat May 13, 1966.

196 60-0428   F-105D
POLLYANA of the 388th TFS. She was the first THUD to reach 3, 000 airframe hours. Flew over 500 missions before being lost over RP1 on September 19, 1968. Major E.R Capling listed as MIA. During her combat service she also carried the name **CAJUN QUEEN.**

197 60-0429   F-105D
Crashed at Korat due to flame out June 14, 1966.

198 60-0430   F-105D
Lost November 7, 1967, to AAA over RP6. Major William Diehl Jr. later died in a POW prison. (Richard Franke)

196▼

198▼

199 60-0431 F-105D
Lost to enemy action over Laos on October 27, 1966. Major R.E. Kline was rescued.

200 60-0432 F-105D
Nicknamed **FARTIN MARTIN** while serving in Thailand. She crashed September 14, 1973, due to drag chute problems. At the time she was serving with the 121st TFS of the D.C. Air National Guard. (Miller)

201 60-0433 F-105D
Crashed October 9, 1967, near McConnell AFB. (See 60- 489)

202 60-0434 F-105D
DAMN YOU CHARLIE BROWN, shot down by a MiG-21 over RP6 on October 9, 1967. Major James A Clements ejected to become a POW. (KAHS)

203 60-0435 F-105D
Lost November 29, 1969, over Thailand due to mid-air collision with F-105 (61-0196) during refueling operations. Photo of artwork from the 34th TFS, 388th TFW. Also carried the name **SATISFACTION** while serving with the same unit. (USAF/Robert D.Archer)

204 60-0436 F-105D
Assigned to the 36th TFS at Bitburg, Germany. She crash landed at Korat on April 25, 1968. At the time of her demise she was called **REBECCA.** (Minert Collection)

205 60-0437 F-105D
She was lost over RP5 on August 21, 1967, during a mission to the Yen Vinh RR Yard. Lt. L.K. Powell was killed in action.

200 ▲

203 ▼   202 ▲   204 ▼

206▲

207▲

209▲

210▲

211▲

212▲

▼213

206 60-0438   F-105D
Shown in the colors of the 22nd TFS, 36th TFW at Bitburg. After her service career she was retired to the storage facility in July 1973. (Isham)

207 60-0439   F-105D
Shown in the colors of the 36th TFW, Bitburg, 1965. Crashed June 2, 1966, while serving at McConnell AFB. (Westersotebier)

208 60-0440   F-105D
Lost to AA January 15, 1967. Captain Gerald Hawkins ejected and was rescued.

209 60-0441   F-105D
Hit by AAA over RP6 on July 19, 1967. Captain W.N. Johnson ejected after crossing the coast and was rescued. (USAF/Byler)

210 60-0442   F-105D
Hit by AA over RP1 on April 20, 1966. Captain J.B. Abernathy was rescued. (Strnad)

211 60-0443   F-105D
Shot down March 11, 1967. Captain Charlie Green ejected over RP6 and was captured. Photographed (Left) while serving with the 36th TFS at Bitburg. (Via Robert D. Archer)

212 60-0444   F-105D
Leaving for a mission on June 19, 1967, while serving with the 44th TFS. Shot down October 7, 1967, over RP6. Major W.E. Fullam was killed in action. (Larsen)

213 60-0445   F-105D
Serving with the 44th TFS she was known as **ENTROPHY MACHINE, GIDDY-UP-GO**, and later **SPARTAN**. Her service life over, she is preserved at Silver Hill, Maryland. Credited with a MiG 17 kill June 3, 1967, by Captain Ralph Kuster. (Larsen)

214 60-0446   F-105D
Crashed July 20, 1961, during delivery from production.

217▲

▲215   218▲

215   60-0447   F-105D
Hit by AA over RP5, crashed in Laos, April 14, 1967. Major Paul Craw rescued.

216   60-0448   F-105D
Collided with 60-0534 near El Dorado, Kansas, July 10, 1968, causing it to crash.

217   60-0449   F-105D
Photographed at Da Nang RVN in September 1966. While serving with the 388th TFW she carried the names **BOUNTY HUNTER, JOSE SHILLE-LAGH,** and **THE BLUE FOX.** She later served with the Virginia Air National Guard. (Geer)

218   60-0450   F-105D
Wearing the colors of the 36th TFW. Lost to AAA on July 13, 1967, while serving with the 357th TFS at Takhli. Major Osborne ejected and was rescued.

219   60-0451   F-105D
Credited with a MiG kill, she was shot down by AA over Laos on April 20, 1970. Captain D.F. Mahan was listed as MIA. Nicknamed **LITTLE LANCER, BILLIE BABE II**. (Griffen)

219▼

220▲

221▲

220 60-0452   F-105D
Serving with the Kansas Air National Guard. Later known as **REBEL RAIDER** while serving with the Virginia Air National Guard. (Minert Collection)

221 60-0453   F-105D
Shown in the colors of the 36 TFW. She was known as **YANKEE AIR PIRATE** in the 388th TFW. Hit by groundfire over RP4, she crash landed at Udorn and was scrapped July 18, 1966. Lt. G.H. Comfer received minor injuries. (Bylers)

222 60-0454   F-105D
Lost to enemy action over RP6 July 5, 1967. Captain W.V. Fredrick was killed in action. (USAF/Robert D.Archer)

223 60-0455   F-105D
On the ramp at Takhli in August 1970. At this time she was known as **CARO- LINA THUNDER.** During her combat career she was also known as **MAT- ZOH BALL SPECIAL** and **KAY'S BABY.** She later received the T-Stick update and served with the 23rd TFW at McConnell AFB, Kansas. (Soldeus)

▼ 222   223▼

224   60-0456   F-105D
Crashed at Bitburg September 5, 1961.

225   60-0457   F-105D
Crashed near Eglin AFB, April 29, 1966.

226   60-0458   F-105D
On the ramp at Korat, July 20, 1969, while serving with the 44th TFS. She was credited with 3 kills during her wartime service. She was known by various nicknames including **SWEET LINDA**, **ANDY CAPP**, **WHITE LIGHTNING COOTER**, and **HERR KLEINES MANS**. Later received the T-Stick modification.(Minert Collection)

227   60-0459   F-105D
Crashed near Nellis AFB December 18, 1968, while serving with the 4520th CCTW. (USAF)

228   60-0460   F-105D
Lost June 29, 1966, on a mission to the Hanoi POL storage area. Captain Murphy Jones ejected and was taken POW. (Byler)

229   60-0461   F-105D
Shown at Nellis AFB while serving with the 4525 FWW in 1967. She was written off due to a main gear failure on October 16, 1967. (Minert Collection)

230 60-0462   F-105D
THE HUNTRESS serving with the 34th TFS. Crashed on take off March 26, 1968, when the right main tire blew.

226▲

227▼

228▲

◄229

▼230

232 ▲

233 ▲

234 ▲

231 60-0463 F-105D
Crashed March 7, 1962, near Lauterbach, Germany, due to engine lubrication problems.

232 60-0464 F-105D
Modified with the T-Stick bombing system. During her combat days she carried the names **M.J.** and **DEE DEE II** with the 544th TFS. (M. Campbell)

233 60-0465 F-105D
Shown while serving with the 457th TFS at Carswell, AFB. (M.Campbell)

234 60-0466 F-105D
Wearing the colors of the 22nd TFS, 36th TFW at Bitburg, Germany, in 1961.Crashed near Chateauroux, France, September 29, 1965, killing Captain George Beran. (Powell)

235 60-0467 F-105D
Crashed December 2, 1961, near Bitburg, Germany.

236 60-0468 F-105D
(First aircraft) Shown in the colors of the 36th TFW at Bitburg. Crashed June 16,1966, while serving with the 23rd TFW at McConnell AFB. (Byler)

235 ▼

236 ▼

237▲

238▲

237 60-0469   F-105D
Lost November 2, 1966, over RP5.
Major R.E. Kline MIA. (Republic)

238 60-0470   F-105D
Assigned to the 36th TFW Bitburg during the early sixties. Attritted April 20,
1967. (Byler)

239 60-0471   F-105D
Shown with the T-Stick modification
while serving with the 23rd TFW at
McConnell AFB in April 1971. (Minert
Collection)

240 60-0472   F-105D
Serving with the D.C. Air National
Guard at Andrews AFB July 10, 1975.
Crashed April 26, 1977, at Byrd Air-
port, VA. (Author's Collection)

241 60-0473   F-105D
First aircraft in line serving with the 36th
TFW at Bitburg. Lost March 23, 1966,
over Laos. Lt K.D. Thomas was rescued. (Griffen)

242 60-0474   F-105D
Crashed January 14, 1964, while serving with the 36th TFW, Bitburg, Germany.

239 ▲

240▼

241▼

243 ▲

246 ▲

243 60-0475 F-105D
After being modified to T-Stick standards, this aircraft crashed onJune 13, 1980, near Bonneville, Utah. (Miller)

244 60-0476 F-105D
Crashed August 1967 at Bitburg, Germany. (See 60-0468, 60-0476 is the second aircraft in line.)

245 60-0477 F-105D
Crashed September 13, 1962, near Maudel, Norway.

246 60-0478 F-105D
Crashed January 28, 1968, due to engine failure. Serving with the 355th TFW at Takhli at the time of the crash. (Strnad)

247 60-0479 F-105D
Crashed March 14, 1962, near Epinal, France.

248 60-0480 F-105D
Known as **AVENGER II** while with the 333th TFS. She was updated with the T-Stick conversion. (Minert Collection)

249 60-0481 F-105D
Serving with the Kansas Air National Guard. This aircraft crashed near Leon, Kansas, on October 2, 1975. (Minert Collection)

248 ▲

249 ▼

250▲

253▲

250 60-0482   F-105D
Enroute to Bitburg, Germany, in 1961.
Later she carried the names **THE
SALTY DOG** and **IRON BUTTERFLY**
while serving with the 388th TFW. She
is preserved in a place of honor at the
Air Force Academy. (Powell)

251 60-0483   F-105D
Lost to AA fire over RP1 October 1,
1966. Captain Cowan Nix taken POW.

252 60-0484   F-105D
First assigned to the 36th TFW at
Bitburg,Germany. Crashed near
Wheelus AB, Libya, due to inflight fire
September 1,1964.

253 60-0485   F-105D
Shot down by AA over RP2 June 16,
1967. Lt/Col. WIlliam Janssen ejected
and was rescued. (USAF)

254 60-0486   F-105D
(Right) Serving with the 36th TFW at
Bitburg. Hit by AA over RP1, July 4,
1966. Lt. B.L. Minton managed to fly
his aircraft out to sea before ejecting.
He was picked up. (Kuykendall)

255 60-0487   F-105D
First aircraft on right. Lost to AA fire
over RP1 on November 6, 1966. Captain Victor Vizcarra was rescued.
(Griffen)

256 60-0488   F-105D
Shown in the colors of the Kansas Air
National Guard in October 1972. Dur-
ing her combat service she carried the
names **AQUARIUS, QUANTUM ME-
CHANIC, THE VIRGIN, BLUE FOX ,
MY ASS IS DRAGON/THE SPANISH
FLY,** and **SCHMOO'S MAGOO**. She
crashed July 3, 1974. (KAHS)

257 60-0489   F-105D
(L)While serving with the 36th TFW.
Shot down by a MiG 21 over RP5 on
January 14, 1968, during a mission to
the Yen Bai Airfield. Major S.H. Horne
MIA. (Byler)

254 ▲   **▼ 255**

256▲

▼ 257

258 60-0490   F-105D
Carrying the tail code for the 354th TFS. She was known as **CAPTAIN RADIO/NUK EM**. Later updated with the T-Stick System. Crashed near Tinker AFB, OK, September 20, 1980. (Hornacki)

259 60-0491   F-105D
Shown in the colors of the 36th TFW at Bitburgh in early 1966. Crashed near McConnell AFB September 24,1967. (Byler)

260 60-0492   F-105D
Serving with the 149th TFS, 192nd TFG VIrginia Air National Guard on October 23,1979. During her service with the unit she was known as **YE OLD WAR HORSE**. (Minert Collection)

261 60-0493   F-105D
Updated with the T-Stick system and serving with the 457th TFS, 506th TFG at Carswell she was retired to AMARC. (Minert Collection)

262 60-0494   F-105D
MR. PRIDE of the 469th TFS. Shot down July 2, 1967, by AA fire over RP2. Captain D.M. Pichard Rescued.

263 60-0495   F-105D
Lost September 5, 1966, over RP1. Captain T.D. Dobbs was rescued after he ejected.

258▲

259▼

260▲

261▼

262 ▼

264 ▲

265 ▲

266 ▲   267 ▶

264   60-0496   F-105D
Serving with the 121st TFS, D.C. Air
National Guard at Andrews, July 11,
1975. (Minert Collection)

265   60-0497   F-105D
MR T, shot down by a MiG 21 over
RP5, November 18, 1967, during a
mission to Phuc Yen Airfield. L/Col. W.N
Reed ejected over Laos and was res-
cued. (Larsen)

266   60-0498   F-105D
Known as **BOOBS** with the 333rd TFS
she was later known as **TOP DOG** with
the Virginia Air National Guard Credited with a MiG 17 kill April 30, 1967.

267   60-0499   F-105D
Serving with the 36th TFW at Bitburg.
Hit by a SAM over RP6 on August 7,
1966. Captain John Wendell was captured. (Kuykendall)

268 ▲

269 ▲

270 ▲

268 60-0500   F-105B
Serving with the 563rd TFS, 23rd TFW McConnell AFB July 10, 1972. Preserved at the Pate Museum of Transportation, Ft. Worth, Texas.

269 60-0501   F-105B
Crashed at Takhli March 11, 1968, due to loss of oil pressure in the engine. Credited with a MiG 17 kill May 13, 1967. (Griffen)

270 60-0502   F-105B
Wearing the colors of the 36th TFW at Bitburg. She was shot down by a MiG 21 over RP5 on December 14, 1966, Captain R.B. "Spade" Cooley was rescued. (Minert Collection)

271 60-0503   F-105B
First assigned to the 36th TFW at Bitburg. Crashed at McConnell AFB, October 10, 1969. (Strnad)

272 60-0504   F-105B
Named **MEMPHIS BELLE II** after the World War 2 B-17. She was credited with two Mig kills. Shown here on the ramp at Takhli between missions. She is preserved at the Air Force Museum. (Minert Collection)

271 ▼

272 ▼

▲273   276▲   ▼279

273   60-0505   F-105D
Shot down by AAA fire Feruary 18, 1969, over Laos. Captain John Brucher was Killed In Action. She carried this artwork and was known as **25 TON CANARY** with the 388th TFW. Also known as **THE TAR HEEL** and **FIGHTING IRISHMAN**. (USAF)

274   60-0506   F-105D
Lost to AA fire March 11, 1967, over RP6. Major Jim Hiteshew was captured.

275   60-0507   F-105D
Crashed July 19, 1961, near St. James, NY, due to controls locking up.

276   60-0508   F-105D
Leading a sister THUD from the 36th TFW. Displayed at Wings over Rockies Museum, Lowry AFB. (Minert Collection)

277   60-0509   F-105D
Crashed September 23, 1963, at Bittburg, Germany.

278   60-0510   F-105D
Crashed April 9, 1963, due to Toss Bomb Computer failure near Suippes Range, France.

279   60-0511   F-105D
Shown in the colors of the 49th TFW. Shot down May 30, 1968, over Laos. Col. N.P. Phillips ejected and was rescued. She carried the name **SWEET SAL** while serving with the 388th TFW. (Minert Collection)

280▲   ▼281

280   60-0512   F-105D
THE MERCENARY from the 34th TFS ready to leave Korat for another mission. Shot down September 1, 1968. Captain D.K. Thaete was rescued. (Larsen)

281   60-0513   F-105D
Shown at Phalsbough, France, in May 1962 while serving with the 49th TFW. Crashed in June1978 near Carswell AFB, Texas while serving with the 457th TFS. She had been modified to T-Stick configuration. (Paulson)

282 ▲

283 ▲

285 ▲

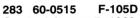

282 60-0514   F-105D
Shown while serving with the Kansas Air National Guard May 9, 1978. (Rotramel)

283 60-0515   F-105D
Crashed August 7, 1968, while serving with the 23rd TFW at McConnell AFB, Kansas. (Robert D. Archer)

284 60-0516   F-105D
First assigned to the 36th TFW at Bitburg. Shot down over RP1 on March 26, 1967. Major Jack Spillers was rescued.

285 60-0517   F-105D
She was called **OTIS** while serving with the 357th TFS. Later modified with the T-Stick system. (Loomis)

286 60-0518   F-105D
Ready for another mission from Korat in 1968. Later shot down over Laos on July 15, 1969. Major R.E. Kennedy was rescued. Credited with a MiG 17 kill December 4, 1966. Nicknamed **THUD PROTECTOR OF SEA/BILLIE BABE**. (USAF)

287 60-0519   F-105D
Photographed in the markings for the 121st TFS D.C. Air National Guard. (Minert Collection)

286 ▼

287 ▼

288 60-0520   F-105D
Crashed January 21, 1964, 40 miles
west of Wheelus AFB, Libya.

289 60-0521   F-105D
Photographed at Hill AFB, April 7, 1973,
while serving with the 457th TFS.
Crashed near Marlow, OK, December
22, 1976. (Knowles)

290 60-0522   F-105D
Enroute to a target in April 1968 while
serving with the 388th TFW. Shot down
September 14, 1968, over RP1/Laos.
Captain D.M. Tribble was rescued af-
ter ejecting. Credited with a MiG 17 kill
May 13, 1967. (USAF/Robert D. Ar-
cher)

291 60-0523   F-105D
Shot down over RP1, August 22, 1966.
Captain Norman Wells was taken
POW.

292 60-0524   F-105D
Shown in 49th TFW markings. This aircraft crashed July 9, 1962, near Spangdahlem.

293 60-0525   F-105D
Serving with the 4520th Combat Crew
training Wing in June 1962. (Isham)

294 60-0526   F-105D
Taking off for another training mission
with the D.C. Air National Guard. Later
known as **WILL-E COYOTE**, while
serving with the D.C. Air National
Guard. Crashed July 11, 1980 while
serving with the 457th TFS. (Minert
Collection)

295 60-0527   F-105D
Shown at Tinker AFB while serving
with the 457th TFS. (Trump)

289▲

290▼

291▲

292▲

293▲

294▼

295▼

296 60-0528   F-105D
Photographed May 10, 1964, while serving with the 36th TFW at Bitburg. (Minert Collection)

297 60-0529   F-105D
Crashed at Nellis AFB November 4, 1966.

298 60-0530   F-105D
Known as **TANDEM TURTLE** while serving with the 34th TFS. She was lost to groundfire over Laos. Lt. J.L. Devoss was rescued. (Larsen)

299 60-0531   F-105D
Photographed at George AFB in June 1962. Crashed near Nellis AFB March 14, 1967. (Isham)

300 60-0532   F-105D
Crashed near Bakersfield, California, October 14, 1968. (Strnad)

301 60-0533   F-105D
Know as **PLAYBOY, SUSAN II THE PLEASURE MACHINE** while serving with the 354th TFS at Takhli. Shown in the colors of the 457th TFS at Carswell AFB in1980 after conversion to the T-Stick configuration. (Minert)

302 60-0534   F-105D
Crashed July 10, 1968, after mid-air collision with F-105D 60-0448 near El Dorado, KS.

▲ 296   298▲

299▲

300▼

301▼

303▲

▼ 305

303 60-0535 F-105D
Photographed at Richard Grabers AFB October 8, 1968. At the time she was serving with the 23rd TFW based at McConnell AFB. She was retired at Keesler AFB in October, 1978. (Gerdes)

304 60-5374 F-105D
Crash landed at Da Nang AFB after being hit by AAA over RP1. Captain W.G. Carey survived. (See 60-0523)

305 60-5375 F-105B
Serving with the 563rd TFS, 23rd TFW in May 1972. She was known as **THE BALD EAGLE**. Also was the personal mount of Colonel Clarence Anderson. At that time she was known as **OLD CROW**. Crashed near Wichita Falls, TX, after mid-air collision with 60-0513 on February 9, 1974.

306 60-5376 F-105D
Serving with the 563rd TFS, 23rd TFW at McConnell AFB April 1973. She carried the names **RUM RUNNER** and **EXCEDRIN HEADACHE # 105**. She crashed in March 1977 near Nellis AFB. (Miller)

307 60-5377 F-105D
Crashed August 27, 1962, near Hopsten, Germany.

308 60-5378 F-105D
Crashed March 19, 1962, near Wheelus AB, Libya, due to fire in forward fuselage.

309 60-5379 F-105D
First assigned to the 49th TFW at Spangdahlem Crashed April 29, 1969, while serving at McConnell AFB, KS.

310 60-5380 F-105D
Crashed October 19, 1967, at Nellis AFB while serving with the 4520 th CCTW.

311 60-5381 F-105D
Lost to AAA over Laos June 14, 1969. Major H. Kahler is listed as MIA. Nicknamed **MISS MARIE** while serving with the 388th TFW. (USAF/R.D.Archer)

306▼

311▼

▲312   314▲

312 60-5382   F-105D
Shown at Bitburg serving with the 36th TFW. Shot down July 19, 1966, by AA over Laos. Captain R.E. Steere was rescued. (Bylers)

313 60-5383   F-105D
Crashed December 15, 1961, during production delivery flight.

314 60-5384   F-105D
Returning from a mission in August 1967. Shot down by a MiG 21 on February 4, 1968. Captain Carl Lasiter was captured. (Caldwell)

315 60-5385   F-105D
On the ramp at Bitburg while serving with the 36th TFW. She was known as **FIREBALL EXPRESS** while serving with the Virginia Air National Guard. (Minert Collection)

316 61-0041   F-105D
Serving with the D.C Air National Guard October 28, 1978. (Miller)

317 61-0042   F-105D
Photographed during a stop at Da Nang RVN in September 1966. At the time she was serving with the 388th TFW. Shot down July 5, 1967, over RP6 on a mission to the Vu Chua RR Yard. Major Ward Dodge died while a POW. (Geer)

315▲

316▼

317 ▲

319▲

318   61-0043   F-105D
First assigned to the 49th TFW at Spangdahlem. Crashed August 14, 1967, 29 miles north of Roswell NM. Colonel Chester Van Etten ejected .

319   61-0044   F-105D
On the ramp with the colors of the 49th TFW in about 1966. (Snyder)

320   61-0045   F-105D
Shot down July 27, 1966, over RP1. Captain James Mitchell ejected and was rescued.

321   61-0046   F-105D
Crashed near Lindsborg, Kansas, October 18, 1966, due to fuel problems. (Strnad)

322   61-0047   F-105D
Photographed at Eglin AFB on June 10, 1970. At the time she was assigned to the 419th TFS, 23rd TFW based at McConnell AFB, Kansas. Crashed March 21, 1978, near Ft. Sill, OK, due to engine problems. (Morris)

323   61-0048   F-105D
Lost over RP6, April 23, 1966, during a mission to the Phu Lang Thuong Bridge. Major B.J. Goss was Killed In Action.

324   61-0049   F-105D
Crashed March 6, 1962, near Wheelus AFB, Libya.

321▲

322▼

▲326   328▲

325   61-0050   F-105D
Photographed at Hickam FIeld in May 1970. She was on her way to the 388th TFW, Korat . She survived the war and later 'served with the Virginia Air National Guard.

326   61-0051   F-105D
Lost to a SAM April 24, 1966, over RP6. Lt/Col. William Cooper listed as MIA. (Strnad)

327   61-0052   F-105D
Crashed May 8, 1962, near Merzig, Germany.

328   61-0053   F-105D
Shot down December 6, 1968, over Laos. Captain R.M. Walker was rescued. (Bylers)

329   61-0054   F-105D
In the markings of the 12th TFS, 18th TFW. Shot down May 23, 1965, over RP3. Major R.F. Herman was rescued. (Minert Collection)

330   61-0055   F-105D
12th TFS, 18th TFW. Carried the nickname **DOROTHY II**. Lost to enemy action over RP1, June 18, 1968. Major C.B. Light was rescued. (Minert Collection)

325▲

329▼

330▼

331▲

332 ▲

334 ▲

331 61-0056 F-105D
Serving with the 121st TFS, 133rd TFW, D.C. Air National Guard, Andrews AFB July 1977. (Mayer)

332 61-0057 F-105D
Lost to enemy action over RP1, October 21, 1966. Captain D.J. Earil listed as MIA. (USAF)

333 61-0058 F-105D
Crashed near Spangdahlem, Germany,   April 26, 1966.

334 61-0059 F-105D
From the 23rd TFW at McConnell AFB, November 1967. Crashed near Lake Isabella, CA, December 8, 1967. (Geer)

335 61-0060 F-105D
From the 354th TFS, 355th TFW March 1965. Shot down over Laos November 24, 1969. Captain J.B. White Killed In Action. (Steigers)

336 61-0061 F-105D
Photographed at Tinker AFB during service with the 465th TFS. (Loomis)

337 61-0062 F-105D
Shot down over RP2, November 18, 1965. Captain L.C. Mahaffey was rescued.

335 ▼

336▼

▲338   339 ▲

338 61-0063   F-105D
At McConnell AFB, April 21, 1972, in the markings of the 23rd TFW. (Rotramel)

339 61-0064   F-105D
Shown in the markings of the 457th TFS, 301st TFW. During her combat service with the 355th TFW she carried the names **PUNKIN II/WILLY**. (Trump)

340 61-0065   F-105D
Serving with the Kansas Air National Guard in May 1978.

341 61-0066   F-105D
Crashed December 21, 1966, near McConnell AFB.

342 61-0067   F-105D
Crashed at El Uotia Range, Libya, March 8, 1965.

343 61-0068   F-105D
Lost to AAA over RP6 on January 5, 1968. Captain William E.Jones listed as KIA. Nicknamed **BARBARA E**.

344 61-0069   F-105D
Credited with one MiG 17 kill on June 3, 1967, she was known as **PUSSY GALORE** and later **CHERRY GIRL** while serving with the 355th TFW. She is preserved at the San Bernadino Air Museum. (Minert Collection)

340▲

341▼

344▼

345▲

346▲

347▲

345 61-0070 F-105D
In service with the 4519th Combat Crew Training Squadron at McConnell AFB in May 1972. Crashed due to in-flight fire September 10, 1973.

346 61-0071 F-105D
Serving with the Kansas Air National Guard on May 1972. During her combat service she was called **COMMIE STOMPER**. Later while serving with the Virginia Air Guard she was known as **REGAL BEAGLE**.

347 61-0072 F-105D
Lost over Laos on January 11, 1969. Major W.M. Thompson was rescued.

348 61-0073 F-105D
Sitting on the ramp while serving with the Kansas Air National Guard. She is preserved at Langley AFB.

349 61-0074 F-105D
High over Germany while serving with the 49th TFW at Spangdahlm. Later received the T-Stick Modification. (Isham)

348 ▼

349▼

350 61-0075   F-105D
Shown in her early service life after receiving her war paint. Later modified with the T-Stick conversion. (Soldeus)

▲ 350   351▲

351 61-0076   F-105D
Shown after receiving the T-Stick Modification and serving with the 457th TFS in August 1971. She was known as **CAVALIER** and **THE ROBIN** during her tenure with the 544th TFS, 355th TFW. (Bracken)

352 61-0077   F-105D
Over a solid undercast, this 49th TFW THUD flies another training sortie. Crashed August 14, 1968. (McNeil)

353 61-0078   F-105D
SITTING PRETTY prepares to leave the line at Korat for another mission. She was lost September 3, 1967, on a mission to the Xom Cul Highway Bridge. Captain H.W. Moore is listed as MIA. (Larsen)

354 61-0079   F-105D
Crashed near Wichita, Kansas, October 23, 1969, due to an inflight fire. (USAF)

355 61-0080   F-105D
On the ramp at McConnell while serving with the 547th TFS. She was the prototype for the T-Stick modification program. (Minert Collection)

352 ▲

353▼   354▼

355 ▲

357 ▲

356   61-0081   F-105D
Crashed near Spangdahlem, Germany, July 28, 1964.

357   61-0082   F-105D
Taking on a load of fuel while serving with the 4th TFW. Shot down September 20, 1965 over RP2. Captain Willis Forby was taken prisoner. (Minert Collection)

358   61-0083   F-105D
Crashed May 6, 1968, while serving with the 479th TFW.

359   61-0084   F-105D
Shown in the markings of the 465th TFS, 507th TFG. She carried the name **PORKY'S PIG** at one time. (Minert Collection)

360   61-0085   F-105D
Lost to AA September 4, 1966, during a mission to the Nguyen Khe POL Storage area. Lt. Thomas McNish became a POW. (USAF/Robert D. Archer)

361   61-0086   F-105D
Serving with the Virginia Air National Guard July 29, 1978. She carried the nickname **YANKEE DOOD IT** at this time. During her service with the 388th TFW at Korat she was known as **DON'T TREAD ON ME** and **BETTY LOU**. (Miller)

359 ▲

360 ▼

361 ▼

362 61-0087   F-105D
Crashed December 20, 1962, near Beuschelab, Germany due to a flame-out.

363 61-0088   F-105D
BALLS 88 in the marking of the 563rd TFS, 23rd TFW at McConnell AFB, Kansas in July 1972. She is preserved at Grissom AFB, Indiana.

364 61-0089   F-105D
Lost over Laos December 21, 1968. Captain Richard Allee was listed MIA. Shown on the right of formation. (Meyerson)

365 61-0090   F-105D
Shot down December 20, 1965, on a mission to the Vu Chua RR Bridge. Captain J.S.Ruffo was rescued.

366 61-0091   F-105D
First assigned to the 4th TFW in February 1962. Operational loss July 8, 1964. Collided with a KC-135 during refueling. Crashed near Ft.Irwin, California, killing the pilot.

367 61-0092   F-105D
Nicknamed **JOHNNY REB** while serving with the 388th TFS. Written off November 17, 1968.

368 61-0093   F-105D
Serving with the D.C.Air National Guard in April 1971. Carried the nicknames **HONEY BEE**, **HONEY BABE**, and **GOOD VIBRATIONS**. Later called **THE NERD BIRD** while serving with the National Guard. (Minert Collection)

369 61-0094   F-105D
Lost to AAA over RP6 during mission to the Dai Loy RR Bypass on November 8, 1967. Captain L.G. Evert was Killed In Action.

370 61-0095   F-105D
(See 61-0057 for photo) Shot down over RP-1 March 24, 1966. Captain Robert E. Bush was killed.

371 61-0096   F-105D
Shown in the markings of the 457th TFS, 301st TFW, after her T-Stick Modification. (Mills)

372 61-0097   F-105D
Assigned to the 49th TFW at Spangdahlem March 22, 1962. Crashed September 26, 1965.

373 61-0098   F-105D
Lost over RP3, August 3, 1965. Major J.E. Bower listed KIA.

363▲

368▼   364▲

▲ 371

374 61-0099   F-105D
On the ramp at Tinker AFB, Oklahoma City, while serving in the reserve unit. Later preserved at Aurora, IL.

375 61-0100   F-105D
Serving with the 457th TFS, 301st TFW. She was known as **HOT STUFF** during service with the 357th TFS, 355th TFW. (Harris)

376 61-0101   F-105D
Crashed May 27, 1963, while serving with the 99th TFW at Spangdahlem, Germany.

◀ 374

▼ 375

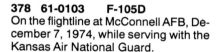
▲ 377   378▲

377   61-0102   F-105D
Shown after her Crash January 24, 1962, at Farmingdale, NY. (Newsday)

378   61-0103   F-105D
On the flightline at McConnell AFB, December 7, 1974, while serving with the Kansas Air National Guard.

379   61-0104   F-105D
Crashed in Laos after being hit by AAA on March 17, 1969. Lt. D.T. Dinan listed as KIA.

380   61-0105   F-105D
Shot down over RP1 May 8, 1967, Captain Michael K. McCuistion was taken POW. (Chesley)

381   61-0106   F-105D
Serving with the Kansas Air National Guard December 7, 1974. She was the last F-105D-15RE built.

382   61-0107   F-105D
Serving with the Kansas Air National Guard March 30, 1977. She is preserved at Kirkland AFB.

383   61-0108   F-105D
Serving with the 562nd TFW, 23rd TFW at McConnell AFB July 10, 1972. She carried the name **KOMBAT KATHY** during her combat service. Preserved at Lackland AFB.

380▲

381▼

382▼

383 ▲

384 ▲

384 61-0109 F-105D
Photographed December 30, 1967, with the 355th TFW. At the time she was known as **BIG KAHUNA**. Lost over Laos March 2, 1969. Major C.C. Bogiages MIA. (Burgess/ Robert D. Archer)

385 61-0110 F-105D
At McConnell AFB after her return from Southeast Asia. Preserved at Brookes AFB, Texas. (Loomis)

386 61-0111 F-105D
Shown serving with the 23rd TFW atMcConnell AFB in November, 1967. Crashed December 5, 1969, near Marquette, KS. (Geer).

387 61-0112 F-105D
Hit by AAA over RP6 she went down over Laos trying to get back to Takhli, July 11,1966. Captain R.H. Laney ejected and was picked up.

388 61-0113 F-105D
Shown nearest to camera while refueling. She was lost July 27, 1965. Captain Kile Berg ejected and was taken POW.

389 61-0114 F-105D
Crashed April 30, 1962, into Mobile Bay, Alabama, killing the pilot, Captain James Stiles.

385 ▲

386 ▼

388 ▼

390 61-0115   F-105D
Serving with the 465th TFS, 507th TFG at Tinker AFB, August 18, 1978. (Malerba/Minert Collection)

391 61-0116   F-105D
Lost to groundfire over RP5 July 20, 1966. Col. W.H.Nelson listed as Killed In Action.

392 61-0117   F-105D
First assigned to the 49th TFW in December 1962. Hit by SAM near Ninh Binh RR bridge September 30, 1965. Crashed at RP-4 NV. Lt. Col. Melvin Killian, Jr., KIA.

393 61-0118   F-105D
Serving with the 23rd TFW.Hit by AA over RP1, July 1, 1968. Lt/Col. J. Modica rescued. (via Robert D. Archer)

394 61-0119   F-105D
Lost over Laos August 4, 1966, during Rescap mission. Lt. Allen Rogers ejected as was rescued.

395 61-0120   F-105D
Lost over RP5 May 31, 1966, during a mission to the Yen Bay Complex. Captain M.W. Steen listed as KIA.

396 61-0121   F-105D
Second aircraft in line. Serving with the 23rd TFW. Hit by a MIG 21 over RP6, crashing in Laos trying to get back toTakhli. Major W.L. McClelland was rescued. (USAF)

397 61-0122   F-105D
Hit by a SAM on a mission to the Paul Doumer Bridge on October 27, 1967. Major Bob Stirm was taken POW.

398 61-0123   F-105D
Lost March 19, 1967 over RP1. Lt/Col J.C. Austin listed as MIA.

399 61-0124   F-105D
EIGHT BALL of the 34th TFS ready for a mission. Shot down down November 20, 1967, by a MiG 21 over RP5. Captain William Butler ejected and became a POW.

400 61-0125   F-105D
Crashed May 12, 1965, at Takhli due to engine problems.

401 61-0126   F-105D
Lost October 27, 1967, over RP6 during a mission to Hanoi. Captain Russell Temperley taken POW. She was known as **MISS TEXAS** AND **OL' RED JR**.

402 61-0127   F-105D
From the 36th TFW. Shot down July 5, 1967, over RP6. Major Dewey Waddell was taken POW. (Minert Collection)

403 61-0128   F-105D
Crashed August 14, 1963, near Bitburg, Germany, killing the pilot, Captain Emeal Tipton.

390▲   ▼ 393

394▼

396 ▲

399▲

402 ▲

404 61-0129 F-105D
In the colors of the Sacremento AMA. Later scrapped at Patuxent River, MD. (Minert Collection)

405 61-0130 F-105D
Shot down by a MiG 21 April 30, 1967, over RP5. Captain Joe Abbott taken POW.

406 61-0131 F-105D
First assigned to the 49th TFW in 1962. Crashed July 27, 1965, while flying from Icirlik AB, Turkey.

407 61-0132 F-105D
HANOI SPECIAL. Crashed May 14, 1968, due to a mid-air encounter. Credited with a MiG 17 kill August 23, 1967.

408 61-0133 F-105D
Lost to AA fire over Laos on June 5, 1965. Captain Walter Kosko was rescued.

404 ▼

407▼

409 61-0134   F-105D
Serving with the 149th TFS at Langley AFB, October 13, 1971.

410 61-0135   F-105D
Shot down May 10, 1966, over RP5. Captain Martin Mahrt was rescued.

411 61-0136   F-105D
In the markings of the 36th TFW at Bitburg. Crashed July 6, 1967, at Takhli due to engine failure. (Bylers)

412 61-0137   F-105D
Crashed near Cassoday, KS, October 10, 1968. Lt/Col James Flowers ejected, but died of injuries.

413 61-0138   F-105D
Serving with the D.C. Air National Guard July 11, 1975. She was known as **CHIPMONK** while serving with the 121st TFS. (Minert Collection)

414 61-0139   F-105D
Crashed due to mid air collision with F-105 62-4240 August 3, 1967, at Takhli.

415 61-0140   F-105D
Nicknamed **THE LONE STAR SPECIAL**. Lost to groundfire over RP6 August 7, 1966. Major Willard Gideon ejected and was taken POW. (Malerba)

416 61-0141   F-105D
Crashed December 10, 1968, near Wurzburg, Germany.

417 61-0142   F-105D
Shot down over RP5 May 30, 1966. Captain David Hatcher taken POW.

418 61-0143   F-105D
Shown on a mission while serving with the 355th TFW in April 1965. Crashed November 14, 1967, near Smokey Hill, KS. (Steigers/Isham)

409▲

411▲

415▲

413▼

418▼

419▲

420▲

421▲

422▼

419 61-0144   F-105D
Shown while serving with the 4th TFW September 22, 1962. Crashed November 7, 1964, near Rago, Kansas. (Olson/Robert D. Archer)

420 61-0145   F-105D
Shown in the markings of the 563rd TFS, 23rd TFW stationed at McConnell AFB. In 1980 she carried rather provocative artwork and was known as **MY HONEYPOT**. (Loomis)

421 61-0146   F-105D
Back from a training sortie while serving with the 465th TFS, July 1979. Preserved at Edwards AFB, CA. (Minert Collection)

422 61-0147   F-105D
Shot down May 5, 1966, on a mission to the Cao Nung RR Bridge. Lt. K.D. Thomas was killed in action. (Strnad)

423 61-0148   F-105D
Crashed at sea June 4, 1967, after being hit by groundfire over RP1. Major C.J. Kough was rescued. (Meyerson)

424 61-0149   F-105D
Flamed out and crashed January 2, 1968, over Thailand due to low fuel while returning from a mission.

423▼

425 ▼

426 ▼

425 61-0150   F-105D
Shot down December 8, 1968, over Laos. Lt. R.A. Rex listed as Killed In Action. (Caldwell)

426 61-0151   F-105D
Back from a August, 1966, mission with 87 holes in her hide. Captain B.R. Reinbold was also wounded. Crashed August 9, 1968, while serving with the 23rd TFW. (USAF)

427 61-0152   F-105D
Known as **8-BALL** while serving with the 34th TFS. She was photgraphed at Tinker AFB, Oklahoma City. (Minert Collection)

428 61-0153   F-105D
Ready for another mission in her 469th TFS revetment. Shot down over Laos September 23, 1970. Captain J.W. Newhouse rescued. (Fitzharris)

429 61-0154   F-105D
In the markings of the 121st TFS D.C. Air National Guard. (Dorr/Minert Collection)

427 ▼

428 ▼

429 ▼

430▲

431▲

432▲

434▼

435▼

430 61-0155 F-105D
Serving with the 563rd TFS, 23rd TFW at McConnell AFB. Hit by groundfire and crashed in RP-1 August 8, 1966. Lt. J.R. Casper ejected and was rescued. (Loomis)

431 61-0156 F-105D
Lost over RP6, April 23, 1966. Captain D. Allinson was listed as KIA.

432 61-0157 F-105D
SHIRLEY ANN of the 421st TFS at Korat. Shot down by AAA on mission to Phu Lang Thoung Bridge April 23, 1966. Captain R.E. Dyczkowski listed as MIA. (USAF)

433 61-0158 F-105D
Lost over RP6 July 8, 1966. Lt Ralph Browning taken POW.

434 61-0159 F-105D
Shown in the colors of the 149th TFS, 182nd TFG Virginia Air National Guard March 16, 1980. Carried the names **HAVE GUN WILL TRAVEL** and **HONEYPOT II** during her combat service in Vietnam. Credited with a MiG 17 kill May 12, 1967.(Minert Collection)

435 61-0160 F-105D
Serving with the 49th TFW in September, 1962. Lost June 2, 1966, due to operational accident at Korat RTAFB. (USAF/Robert D. Archer)

▲436   437▲

436 61-0161   F-105D
Serving with the 457th TFS April 25, 1972. Carried the names **ABOVE AND BEYOND/LI'L CHERYL** and **THE OUTLAW** during her service in SEA. (Minert Collection)

437 61-0162   F-105D
Lost over Laos March 17, 1968. Captain T.T. Hensley listed as KIA. She carried this artwork while serving with the 388th TFW. (USAF/Robert D. Archer)

438 61-0163   F-105D
Known as **TOMMY'S HAWK**. Lost over RP4 November 3, 1965. Went out of control when only one 3,000 lb. bomb released, and crashed into a mountainside. Captain Dwight Bowles listed KIA. (Campbell Archives/OKC)

439 61-0164   F-105D
Serving with the Virginia Air National Guard July 29, 1978. During her service with the Virginia Air National Guard she was known as **GOLDEN GUN**. (Geer)

440 61-0165   F-105D
Shown while serving at George AFB, California. She carried the names **SUZY BABY** and **JAKE'S JEWEL** during her combat career. She is preserved at Pope AFB. (Roth)

438▲

439▼

440▼

441▲

443▲

441 61-0166 F-105D
Shown in a rather interesting gray paint job. (John Heyer)

442 61-0167 F-105D
Photographed at Richmond, VA, in April1978. She was known as **MILLARD THE MALLARD** while serving with the Virginia Air National Guard. (Miller)

443 61-0168 F-105D
Lost at sea after taking ground fire damage June 7, 1966, Captain J.F. Bayles was rescued. (Chesley)

444 61-0169 F-105D
At the time of this photo she was serving with the 23rd TFW, 561st TFS, and carried the name **EVERY MAN A TIGER/HAZEL, MOOSE MOBILE**. Shot down October 28, 1967, over RP6. Lt/Col. Tom Kirk taken POW. (Geer)

445 61-0170 F-105D
Known as **THUNDER AX** while serving with the Virginia Air National Guard. Photographed May 3, 1980. Photographed while serving with the 3246th Test Wing at McClelland AFB in June, 1970. (Miller)

442▲

444▼

445▼

446 61-0171   F-105D
Lost over RP1, April 17, 1965. Captain Samuel Woodworth listed as KIA. (Strnad)

446▲

447▲

447 61-0172   F-105D
Lost August 11, 1965, over RP. 3 due to 37mm groundfire. Captain L.E. Wilson ejected and was rescued. Captain L.E. Wilson ejected and was rescued. (Meyerson)

448 61-0173   F-105D
Lost over RP6 November 5, 1967, on a mission to the Phuc Yen Airfield. Captain Billy Sparks ejected and was rescued. (Malerba)

449 61-0174   F-105D
Shown first in the line up of THUDS on the ramp at Tahkli. Lost May 15, 1966. Captain R.C. Balcom listed as MIA. (Chesley)

450 61-0175   F-105D
Shown in the markings of the Kansas Air National Guard December 7, 1974. She is preserved at Sheppard AFB, Texas. (KAHS)

451 61-0176   F-105D
Serving with the Kansas Air National Guard in her final days. She carried the names **THE JOLLY ROGER, PA-TIENCE MY ASS,** and **THE MAX BEAK** during her combat days in SEA. She is preserved at Maxwell AFB, Alabama.

449▲

450▼

451▼

456 ▲

459 ▲

458 ▲

▼ 460

452 61-0177   F-105D
Hit by AAA over RP6. Major William Barthelmas, Jr., was killed when the aircraft crashed in Thailand on July 27, 1965.

453 61-0178   F-105D
Hit by 27mm groundfire over RP1 March 23, 1966. Major R.A. Hill ejected after crossing the Thailand border and was rescued.

454 61-0179   F-105D
Lost to AAA over RP5 May 6, 1966. Lt/Col. James Lamar survived to become a POW.

455 61-0180   F-105D
Lost over RP5 October 13, 1965. Major James Randell was rescued.

456 61-0181   F-105D
Flying for the 44th TFS in November 1963. Lost due to mid air collision October 23, 1976, with F-105D 62-4335. (Isham)

457 61-0182   F-105D
Lost December 1, 1965, over RP6B during mission to the Cao Nung RR Bridge. Captain T.E . Reitman was KIA.

458 61-0183   F-105D
On the ramp at Tinker AFB, Oklahoma City, November 22, 1972. (Loomis)

459 61-0184   F-105D
Hit by groundfire over RP5 on August 10, 1965. Captain M.J. Kelch managed to fly the plane to Laos before ejecting and being rescued. Shown leading the flight.(Campbell Archives/OKC)

460 61-0185   F-105D
Shown beside a sister THUD before the days of dark camouflage paint. Hit by 37mm over RP5 August 31, 1965. Major W.H. Bollinger ejected and was rescued. (Campbell Archives)

461▲

463 ▲

461   61-0186   F-105D
Shot down September 26, 1966, over RP6. Captain Arthur Balard was taken POW. (Bylers)

462   61-0187   F-105D
Hit by a SAM over RP6 on December 13, 1966. Captain S.E. Waters was KIA. (See 61-0184/left wing)

463   61-0188   F-105D
From the 121st TFS, 113th TFG. During her combat years she carried the nickname **STEPHANIE ALLISON**. (Minert Collection)

464   61-0189   F-105D
Lost over RP4, September 16, 1965. Major Ray Merritt ejected and was captured.

465   61-0190   F-105D
Lost June 2, 1967, on a mission to the Kep RR Yard. Major Dewey Smith was captured after ejection.

466   61-0191   F-105D
Crashed in South Vietnam after being hit over RP6 on September 17, 1966. Captain Allen Rutherford was rescued.

467 ▲

468 ▼

467   61-0192   F-105D
First assigned to the 18TFW at Kadena. Crashed May 5, 1966. (USAF)

468   61-0193   F-105D
Shown in the markings of the 563rd TFS 23rd TFW McConnell AFB. Hit by 37 mm near Yen Bay Arsenal August 29, 1965. Crashed in RP-5 NV. Maj. Ronald Byrne ejected to become a POW. (Loomis)

469 ▲

470 ▲

471 ▲

▼ 474

469 61-0194 F-105D
Photographed while serving in the 34th TFS. Known as **THE AVENGER**, she was shot down May 28, 1968. Major Roger Ingvalson was taken POW. (USAF)

470 61-0195 F-105D
Crashed at TakhliOctober 27, 1967, due to an engine fire on take off. (Green)

471 61-0196 F-105D
Crashed November 28, 1969, due to damage suffered during a refueling mid-air collision. Carried nickname **MARY SABRE** in this February, 1968, photo. (Via Robert D. Archer).

472 61-0197 F-105D
Lost August 14, 1966, over RP6. Captain Franklin listed as MIA.

473 61-0198 F-105D
Lost to groundfire over RP6A May 5, 1967. Lt. James Shively ejected and was captured.

474 61-0199 F-105D
Shown in the colors of the 301st TFW. She is preserved at Lackland AFB. (Niedermeir)

475 61-0200 F-105D
Lost over Laos September 21, 1965. Captain Fredrick Greenwood rescued. (See 62-4218. 6th in line)

476 61-0201 F-105D
Lost September 12, 1966, over RP3. Captain Robert Waggoner was captured.

477 61-0202 F-105D
Crashed April 10, 1969, near Andover, KS. Maj. Don Frazier survived.

478 ▲

479 ▲

478 61-0203 F-105D
Crashed May 9, 1963, while serving with the 4th TFW. (Malerba)

479 61-0204 F-105D
Photographed while serving with the 357th TFS 355th TFW where she was known as **THE HUMMER I.** (Miller)

480 61-0205 F-105D
MR. BLACKBIRD of the 34th TFS. Shot down October 17, 1967, on a mission to Dap Cau RR Yard. Captain Anthony Andrews was taken POW.

481 61-0206 F-105D
From the 469th TFS 388th TFW at Korat. Kicks in the AB for take off for another mission. She was lost over RP1 April 15, 1968. Major J. Metz died in a POW Camp.(Geer)

482 61-0207 F-105D
Crashed March 10, 1964, 60 miles NE of Kadena AB. (See 61-0207/rt wing)

483 61-0208 F-105D
MR BULLDOG lost November 19, 1967, to a SAM over RP6A. Captain H.H. Clinck listed as MIA. (Larsen)

484 61-0209 F-105D
Shown in the colors of the 66FWS, 57th FWW, Nellis AFB. Crashed March 20, 1965. (Isham)

480 ▲

▼ 481

483 ▼

490 ▲

◄484

487 ▲

▼492

485 61-0210   F-105D
Lost to AAA January 31, 1966, over RP3. Captain Eugene Hamilton was Killed In Action.

486 61-0211   F-105D
Crashed March 1, 1964, while serving with the 18th TFW at Kadena.

487 61-0212   F-105D
Serving with the Virginia ANG as **THUNDERCHIEF**. She was also known as **PEACE ENVOY** and **RUN-NING GUN V**. (KAHS)

488 61-0213   F-105D
Crashed at sea after being hit by groundfire over RP3, June 15, 1967. Captain J.W. Swanson listed as MIA.

489 61-0214   F-105D
Hit by 37 mm groundfire March 2, 1965. Captain Robert "Boris" Baird was rescued.

490 61-0215   F-105D
Crashed in Laos due to battle damage February 26, 1966. Captain Charles Boyd was rescued. (Campbell Archives /OKC)

491 61-0216   F-105D
Crashed February 7, 1963, while serving with the 4th TFW. Accident caused by a defective bomb fuse. Crashed at Eglin AFB.

492 61-0217   F-105D
Lost to AAA over RP4 on September 16,1965. Lt/Col. Robinson Risner ejected to become a POW.

493 61-0218   F-105D
Crashed September 5, 1964, at Kadena AFB.

▲494   495▲

494 61-0219   F-105D
THE TRAVELLER. Crash landed August 17, 1968. Carried the name **LINDA LOU** and **FOREIGN AID** also during her service in SEA. (Larsen)

495 61-0220   F-105D
Crashed at Takhli April 15, 1970, due to onboard fire. She was known as **I DREAM OF JEANIE** while serving with the 388th TFW at Korat in 1968. (Meyerson)

496 62-4217   F-105D
Shown over snow capped mountains. Lost April 4, 1965, on a mission against the Thanh Hoa Bridge. Major Carlyle Harris ejected to become a POW. (Campbell Archives /OKC)

497 62-4218   F-105D
Crashed November 12, 1965, at Takhli. The accident was fatal for Captain William Miller. (Malerba)

498 62-4219   F-105D
Lost to enemy action over RP 4, March 7, 1966. Captain H.V. Smith listed as MIA.

499 62-4220   F-105D
Shown (flying left wing)in the markings of the 18th TFW at Kadena. Lost to groundfire over RP5 June 14, 1965. Major Larry Guarino ejected to become a POW. (Meyerson)

497 ▲

▼496   499▼

500▲

504▲

505▲

▼508

500   62-4221   F-105D
Nicknamed **THE FIGHTING IRISH-MAN** and **WILD CHILD**. She was lost November 18, 1967, over RP6 after being hit by a SA-2 missile. Colonel Edward Burdett died while serving as a POW. (Minert Collection)

501   62-4222   F-105D
Shot down over RP3, May 17, 1965. Captain J.J. Taliaferro was rescued. (See 62-4218. 9th in line)

502   62-4223   F-105D
Crashed January 22, 1964, while serving with the 4th TFW. The pilot, Captain Phillip Griggs, was fatally injured.

503   62-4224   F-105D
Lost to groundfire over RP6 June 30, 1965. Captain R.K. Nierste ejected and was rescued.

504   62-4225   F-105D
Shown in early aluminum paint and TAC markings. Crashed February 2, 1966. (Authors Collection)

505   62-4226   F-105D
Shown in early markings ready for a mission. Crashed March 8, 1968, near Raymond, KS. (Authors' collection)

506   62-4227   F-105D
Hit by 37/57mm groundfire near La danh Pol storage area July 21, 1966, and crashed in RP5. Captain R. Tiffin listed as KIA.

507   62-4228   F-105D
Known as **PAPA THUD** and **MUTT'S MAN-O-WAR** during her combat life. She later served with the D.C. Air National Guard. She is preserved at Lackland AFB.
(Campbell Archives/OKC)

508   62-4229   F-105D
Nicknamed **JEANIE II, I DREAM OF JEANIE**, and **SNEAKY COYOTE**. She later served with the Virginia ANG. Crashed August 31, 1977, into Pamlico Sound, SC, after engine flame out. (Minert Collection)

509   62-4230   F-105D
Lost over Laos March 16, 1970. Major W.J. Wycoff was rescued.

510▲

513▶

510 62-4231 F-105D
Shot down October 27, 1967, over RP2. Col. John Flynn ejected and was captured. (Minert Collection)

511 62-4232 F-105D
Lost to AAA over RP2 on July 6, 1965. Captain D.I. Williamson listed as MIA.

512 62-4233 F-105D
Crashed at sea after being hit over RP2, March 22, 1965. Lt/Col. Robinson Risner was rescued.

513 62-4234 F-105D
SWEET THIRZA MAY shot down December 24, 1968. Major C.R. Brownlee listed MIA. (Minert Collection)

514 62-4235 F-105D
Lost August 22, 1965, over RP4. Major Dean A. Pogreba was rescued.

515 62-4236 F-105D
Photographed in July 1965. Shot down May 8, 1966, over RP6. Lt. James Ray was taken POW. (Paulson)

516 62-4237 F-105D
Crashed at Kadena AFB, July 26, 1965.

517 62-4238 F-105D
Lost over RP5 September 20, 1965. Captain W.L. Hawkins was KIA.

518 62-4239 F-105D
Shot down by a SA/2 over RP6A January 21, 1967. Lt/Col. Gene Conley KIA.

519 62-4240 F-105D
Crashed August 3, 1967, due to a mid-air with F-105 61-0139. (USAF)

520 62-4241 F-105D
Crashed at Kadena November 24, 1965, while serving with the 18th TFW.

515▲

▼517

519▲

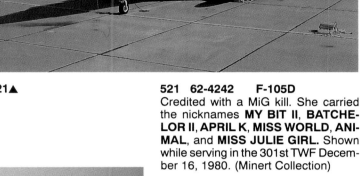

521▲

521 62-4242 F-105D
Credited with a MiG kill. She carried the nicknames **MY BIT II**, **BATCHELOR II**, **APRIL K**, **MISS WORLD**, **ANIMAL**, and **MISS JULIE GIRL.** Shown while serving in the 301st TWF December 16, 1980. (Minert Collection)

522 62-4243 F-105D
Crashed at Korat October 7, 1969, due to fuel starvation. (See 60-0411. On the refueling boom)

523 62-4244 F-105D
From the 121st TFS, 18th TFW landing at Yokota AFB June 3, 1971. Carried the nicknames **LAMAR JEAN II, HIGH STEPPER**. Crashed into the Pacific Ocean April 21, 1972, while serving with the 12th TFS at Kadena AFB. (Tokunaca)

524 62-4245 F-105D
Crashed at Kadena May 13, 1964, 230 miles SE of Okinawa. Pilot was rescued.

525 62-4246 F-105D
Photographed in November 1971 while serving with the 563rd TFS, 23rd TFW. Carried the nickname **THOR'S HAMMER** while with the 357th TFS 355th TFW. (Miller)

526 62-4247 F-105D
Lost over RP5, September 17, 1965, due to groundfire. Lt. D.A. Klenda listed as KIA.

523▲

525▼

526▼

527▲

530▲

527 62-4248 F-105D
Shown while serving with the 456th TFS, at Tinker AFB in June 1973. During her combat service she carried the nicknames **THE GOBBLER** and **LADY LUCK**. This THUD crashed in August 12, 1974. (Geer)

528 62-4249 F-105D
Lost over RP4 August 2, 1965. Captain Robert Doughtrey ejected and became a POW.

529 62-4250 F-105D
Crashed January 23, 1964, at Osan, Korea, while serving with the 18th TFW.

530 62-4251 F-105D
Lost February 19, 1966, over Laos. Captain R.C. Green was rescued. (Strnad)

531 62-4252 F-105D
Nicknamed **VIET NAM ANG** she was shot down July 27, 1965. Captain Robert Purcell was taken POW. (Minert Collection)

532 62-4253 F-105D
Photographed July 21, 1979, while serving with the Kansas Air National Guard. She carried the names **RAJIN CAJUN**, **RYCH BITCH**, and **THUNDER BEE**. She is preserved at McConnell AFB. (Authors' Collection)

533 62-4254 F-105D
Crashed at sea after being hit by AAA over RP1 on July 6, 1966. Captain E.L. Stanford was rescued.

531▲

▼532

534▲

535 ▲

536▲

534 62-4255 F-105D
Lost May 10, 1966, over RP1. Captain J.E. Bailey was killed. (Green)

535 62-4256 F-105D
Lost over Laos February 11, 1969. Lt. R.J. Zukowski is listed as MIA. (USAF)

536 62-4257 F-105D
Shot down July 27, 1965, by AAA over RP5. Captain Walter Kasko listed MIA. (Minert Collection)

537 62-4258 F-105D
Shot down by a SAM November 17, 1967 over RP6. Major C. Edward Cappelli was killed. (See 62-4218. 8th in line)

538 62-4259 F-105D
Serving with the 456th TFS at Tinker AFB in June 1973. She was called **CAJUN QUEEN** while serving with the 333rd TFS. (Geer)

539 62-4260 F-105D
Lost March 2, 1965, over RP1 Major George Panas was rescued.

540 62-4261 F-105D
Lost March 11, 1967, due to SAM hit over RP6. Captain Joe Karin listed as KIA. (See 62-4218. 2nd in line)

▼538   540▼

541   62-4262   F-105D
Lost to AAA over RP6 October 24, 1967, during a mission to the Kep Airfield. Captain M.D. Scott ejected and was rescued.

542   62-4263   F-105D
Crashed September 20, 1963, near Kadena AB.

543   62-4264   F-105D
ROMPIN RUDY from the 34th TFS, 388th TFW. Shot down over RP1 October 27, 1968. Lt. R.C. Edmunds, Jr., was killed. (USAF/Robert D. Archer)

544   62-4265   F-105D
Second from camera. Hit by AAA over Laos January 10, 1967. Captain J.P. Gauley was killed when his chute failed. (Via Robert D. Archer)

545   62-4266   F-105D
Lost to groundfire over RP6 August 14, 1966. Captain John W. Brodak ejected and became a POW. (See 62-4218 3rd in line)

546   62-4267   F-105D
First assigned to the 18th TFW at Kadena. Crashed October 27, 1964, near Yokota AB, Japan.

547   62-4268   F-105D
Shot down August 24, 1967, on a mission to the Lang Dang RR Yard. Captain Jay C. Hess ejected and was taken POW. (See 62-4218. 7th in line)

548   62-4269   F-105D
Serving with the 18th TFW in 1963. Shot down April 3, 1969, over RP6. Major P.B. Christianson was killed. Carried the nick-names **BIG MIKE**, **OKIE JUDY**, **THE IMPOSSIBLE DREAM**, **ON TARGET/PHYLUS I**. (Minert Collection)

549   62-4270   F-105D
Returning from a mission while serving with the 34th TFS 388th TFW. Shot down March 29, 1969, over Laos. Nick named **THE LIQUIDATOR**. She also carried the name **NOLI NON LEGITEME CARBOR UNDEM EST** (Don't Let The Bastards Wear you down).

550   62-4271   F-105D
Shot down July 25, 1966, over RP6. Major F.C. Hiebert was rescued. (Paulson)

551   62-4272   F-105D
Delivered to the 4th TFW March 4, 1963. Crashed near George AFB, California, January 14, 1970, while serving with the 23rd TFW.

552   62-4273   F-105D
Shot down June 8, 1966. Major J.C. Holley was rescued after bailing out. (USAF)

553   62-4274   F-105D
Shot down over Laos March 4, 1967. Major Ralph Carlock KIA.

543▲   ▼ 544

548▼

549▲

▼ 550

552▼

554 62-4275   F-105D
Lost to flak September 9, 1966, over RP6B. Captain John Blevins taken POW.

555 62-4276   F-105D
Crashed September 12, 1964, at Seymour Johnson AFB. (See 62-4218. 5th in line)

556 62-4277   F-105D
Assigned to the 4th TFW March 25, 1963. Crashed near Osan AB, Korea, March 8, 1968.

557 62-4278   F-105D
Lost to enemy action August 12, 1967, over RP6. Captain Thomas Norris taken POW.

558 62-4279   F-105D
Shown while serving with the 465th TFS at Tinker AFB. (Muir)

559 62-4280   F-105D
Shot down over RP6 September 17, 1966. Captain D.D. Leetun ejected and was rescued. (Paulson)

560 62-4281   F-105D
Shot down September 13, 1966. Lt. K.V. Hallmark was rescued.

561 62-4282   F-105D
Shown in the markings of the 4th TFW over Vietnam in December 1965. Shot down July 11, 1966, by AAA over RP6. Captain Lewis Shattuck was taken POW. (USAF)

562 62-4283   F-105B
MISS M NOOKIE of the 44th TFS. Shot down November 18, 1967, by a SA-2 over RP6. Major L.J. Hauer listed as MIA. (Larsen)

563 62-4284   F-105D
Known as **MARY KAY, WAR LOVER/ MIG KILLER** during her combat service. She is credited with three MiG kills. A double kill was achieved on March 10, 1967, by Captain Max Brestel. The third kill was on October 27, 1967, by Captain Gene Basel. (Paulson)

564 62-4285   F-105D
Lost November 28, 1965, over RP5. Captain Jon Reynolds was taken POW.

565 62-4286   F-105D
THE MAD BOMBER from the 469th TFS was lost November 6, 1967, over RP6. Major R.W. Hagerman listed as MIA

566 62-4287   F-105D
Lost over RP6 September 19, 1966. Captain Donald Waltman taken POW. (Paulson)

567 62-4288   F-105D
Crashed at Korat November 10, 1966, due to engine failure. Major Dain Milliman was killed.

557▲   ▲558

559▼

561▲

562▲ ▼563

565▼

566▼

568　62-4289　F-105D
Crashed October 10, 1963, at Seymour Johnson AFB while serving with the 4th TFW.

569　62-4290　F-105D
Lost to enemy action June 8, 1965, over RP2. Captain Harold Rademacher bailed out and was rescued.

570　62-4291　F-105D
Shown at McConnell AFB March 20, 1977. She was retired to AMARC. Shipped to Clark AFB P.I August 1983

571　62-4292　F-105D
Shot down by AAA over RP1 August 9, 1968. Colonel David W. Winn taken POW.

572　62-4293　F-105D
Lost May 11, 1966, over RP1. Captain F.J. Feneley was KIA. (Malerba)

573　62-4294　F-105D
Shot down April 25, 1967, over RP6. Lt. Robert Weskamp listed as MIA. (Paulson)

574　62-4295　F-105D
Shot down over RP6B October 5, 1965. Major Dean Pogreba was killed in action. He was awarded the Air Force Cross.

575　62-4296　F-105D
Lost to enemy action over Laos, January 13, 1965. Captain Albert Vollmer was rescued.

576　62-4297　F-105D
Photographed in May 1964, she was first assigned to the 355th TFW in April 1963. This aircraft crashed February 26, 1965, near Oxford, KS. (Bailey)

577　62-4298　F-105D
Damaged by an encounter with a MiG over RP6, she crashed in route back to Korat on July 27, 1965. Major Jack Farr was killed in action.

578　62-4299　F-105D
Shown while serving with the 466th TFS at Hill AFB, Utah where she carried the name **THE DESERT FOX**. The name was the result of the paint scheme that she carried. (Dienst)

579　62-4300　F-105D
Crashed at Korat in October, 1966, due to engine failure, killing the pilot.

580　62-4301　F-105D
MY KARMA of the 466th TFS photographed October 3, 1981. During combat she was credited with a ground kill of a IL-28. (MacSorley)

570▲　　　▼ 572

573▼

576▲

▼578

580▼

581 62-4302 F-105D
Photographed at Tinker AFB, November 22, 1972. (Loomis)

▲ 581

584 ▲

582 62-4303 F-105D
Crashed at sea after being hit by AAA over RP2 on September 2, 1966. Captain E.R. Skowron was rescued.

583 62-4304 F-105D
Lost over RP6 on April 29, 1966, during a mission to the Thai Nguyen RR Yard. Lt. D.W. Bruch Jr was killed in action.

584 62-4305 F-105D
Lost October 14, 1965, to a MiG over RP5 Captain R.H. Schuller was killed. (USAF)

585 62-4306 F-105D
Hit by groundfire over RP6B September 14, 1966. Lt J.R. Casper bailed out and was rescued. (USAF)

586 62-4307 F-105D
Photographed on the ramp at McConnell AFB, Kansas, July 10, 1972, while serving with the 23rd TFW. Crashed June 27, 1973, near Richmond, VA.

587 62-4308 F-105D
Shot down over RP6 July 20, 1966. Captain M.R. Lewis, Jr was listed MIA. The mission was to the Vu Chua RR Bridge.

585 ▲

586 ▼

588▼

589▲

590▲

588 62-4309 F-105D
The 588th THUD built, she crashed March 12, 1965.

589 62-4310 F-105D
Photographed at Edwards AFB, she crashed June 8, 1965, near Clark AFB due to engine failure. (USAF)

590 62-4311 F-105D
Serving with the 121 TFS at Andrews AFB August 26, 1972. (Miller)

591 62-4312 F-105D
Crashed July 18, 1966, at Korat due to engine failure.

592 62-4313 F-105D
Hit by groundfire over RP6B November 11, 1966. Major Art Mearns listed as MIA.

593 62-4314 F-105D
Photographed July 10, 1972, while serving with the 562nd TFS 23rd TFW (FLYING TIGERS) at McConnell AFB. Crashed August 30, 1972, Nellis AFB. (KAHS)

594 62-4315 F-105D
Shot down August 6, 1966, over RP6. Captain Allen Rutherford ejected and was rescued. (USAF)

593▲
594▼

595 62-4316   F-105D
Hit by groundfire over RP6 June 30, 1967. Major Ralph Kuster ejected over Laos and was rescued.

596 62-4317   F-105D
Crashed May 2, 1963, after a mid-air with 62-4321.

597 62-4318   F-105D
Serving with the Kansas Air National Guard. She was known as **IRON BUTTERFLY** while serving with the 357th TFS during Vietnam. (Loomis)

598 62-4319   F-105D
Crashed in North Vietnam after being hit by AAA June 23, 1965. Major Robert Wilson was rescued. (Strnad)

599 62-4320   F-105D
Hooking up to a tanker while serving with the 12th TFS 18th TFW. She crashed September 28, 1970, while serving with the 18th TFW at Kadena. (Meyerson).

600 62-4321   F-105D
Crashed near Farmingdale N.Y. after a mid-air with F-105 62-4317 May 2, 1963.

601 62-4322   F-105D
Crashed February 11, 1964.

602 62-4323   F-105D
Shot down over RP6A , August 12, 1966, while attacking POL storage. Captain Martin Neuens ejected to become a POW. (USAF)

603 62-4324   F-105D
Crashed at Takhli January 20, 1966, due to engine failure.

604 62-4325   F-105D
Crashed March 14, 1967, due to control failure during a test flight at Korat AB.

597▲

598▼   599▲   602▼

605▲

607▲

608▲

▼611

605 62-4326   F-105D
Shown while serving with the 44th TFS. Shot down October 17, 1967, while attacking the Dap Cau RR Yard, Major D.E. O'dell ejected to become a POW. (Geer)

606 62-4327   F-105D
Hit by AAA over RP5 August 8, 1966. Captain Fredrick Flom ejected and became a POW.

607 62-4328   F-105D
Serving with the 466th TFS Hill AFB, Utah. (Isham)

608 62-4329   F-105D
Serving with the 35th TFS in 1965. Crashed October 5, 1967, at Takhli due to engine failure. (Robert D.Archer)

609 62-4330   F-105D
Hit by AA over RP1 April 19, 1966. Lt. L.A. Adams was KIA.

610 62-4331   F-105D
Shot down by a MiG-17 on December 5, 1966. Major B.N. Begley listed as MIA.

611 62-4332   F-105D
Hit by AAA over RP6B November 16, 1966. The aircraft crashed at sea, killing Captain Donald Green. (Green)

612 62-4333   F-105D
Shot down over RP5 October 14, 1965. Captain Tom Sima ejected and was taken POW.

▲613   614▲

613   62-4334   F-105D
Hit by AAA over RP1 July 28, 1967.
Crashed in Laos while trying to make
it back to Korat. Lt. Karl W. Richter was
rescued . He later died of his injuries.
It was his 198th mission. (USAF)

614   62-4335   F-105D
Crashed October 23, 1967, due to a
midair with 61-0181 near Takhli.

615   62-4336   F-105D
Hit by groundfire over Laos March 6,
1968. Captain Frank Peck ejected over
Laos and was rescued. (Green)

616   62-4337   F-105D
Hit by groundfire over RP1 September
6, 1965. Captain J.T. Clark nursed the
crippled THUD to the Gulf of Tonkin and
ejected. He was rescued.

617   62-4338   F-105D
ALICE'S JOY the personal mount of
Colonel Jack Broughton during his
combat tour with the 355th TFW at
Takhli. The THUD was shot down Sep-
tember 2, 1967, over RP1. Major Will-
iam Bennett was Killed In Action.
(Broughton)

618   62-4339   F-105D
Photographed at Kadena AFB.
Crashed at Kadena February 13, 1964.
(Meyerson)

615 ▲

617▼

618▼

619▲

622▲

619 62-4340 F-105D
Shot down over RP6 April 24, 1966.
Lt. Jerry Driscoll ejected and was taken
POW. (Reid)

620 62-4341 F-105D
Lost to enemy AAA over RP6 September 25, 1966. Captain C.E. Cushman
was KIA.

621 62-4342 F-105D
Hit by a SAM over RP4 November 5,
1965. Lt/Col George C. McCleary was
listed MIA.

622 62-4343 F-105D
Lost to AAA August 8, 1966 over RP5.
Major James Kasler became a POW
on his 91st mission. (USAF)

623 62-4344 F-105D
Shown while serving with the 149th
TFS of the Virginia Air National Guard.
She carried the nicknames **WELFARE
CADILLAC, RITA BABY, THUNDER
PUD**, and **WYOMING THUD**. She was
known as **BATTLIN GATLIN** while
serving with the VANG. (Sullivan)

624 62-4345 F-105D
Crashed February 7, 1964.

625 62-4346 F-105D
Shown in the colors of the 446th TFS
from Hill AFB. She carried the names
GOOD GOLLY MISS MOLLY and
ITAZUKE EXPRESS during her combat service. (Isham)

623▲

▼ 625

626 62-4347 F-105D
Shown at Offut AFB in June 1973, while serving with the 466th TFS. She carried the names **LITTLE LOIS ANN**, **CALAMITY JANE**, and **WENDY JUNE III** during her combat career. She was known as **STAR DUST 6** with the 466th TFS, and then acquired the name **HIGH TIME THUD** due to the fact that she had more airframe hours than any other THUD. (Hill)

627 62-4348 F-105D
Shown at Tinker AFB. Crashed December 9, 1978, 50 miles NNW of Holloman AFB, NM. (Loomis)

628 62-4349 F-105D
Crashed while serving with the 355th TFW at McConnell AFB on December 28, 1964. The accident was caused by engine failure near Maize, Kansas.

629 62-4350 F-105D
Lost to AAA fire over RP4 October 25, 1965. Lt/Col. Fred Cherry ejected and was taken POW.

630 62-4351 F-105D
Written off August 23, 1965, while serving with 36 TFS at Takhli.

631 62-4352 F-105D
Hit by SAM over RP6 May 5, 1967. Lt/Col. Gordon Larson was taken POW. Nicknamed **THUNDERCHIEF**. (2nd on the flightline, USAF)

632 62-4353 F-105D
Shown in the colors of the 466th TFS at Hill AFB, Utah, in July 1982. Carried the name **BILLIE FERN** with the 354th TFS. Nicknamed **NO GUTS NO GLORY** with the 466th TFS.

633 62-4354 F-105D
Lost over RP1 July 1, 1966. Lt. Burton Campbell taken POW.

626 ▲

627 ▲

631 ▲

632 ▼

634▲

635 ▲

637▲

634 62-4355   F-105D
Crashed on take off from Tahkli August 30, 1965.(Plunkett)

635 62-4356   F-105D
Crashed October 28, 1967, at Korat due to an engine problem.

636 62-4357   F-105D
On the boom while refueling. Shot down April 10, 1967, over RP1. Major John O'Grady listed MIA on a mission to Mu Gia Pass. (Isham)

637 62-4358   F-105D
Lost over RP6 due to AAA June 21, 1966. Lt. J.B. Sullivan listed MIA.

638 62-4359   F-105D
TWELVE O'CLOCK HIGH crashed due to flame out September 12, 1968.

636▼

638▼

641▲

643▲

639   62-4360   F-105B
Known as **IRON DUKE**, she is preserved at Tinker AFB. (Franklin)

640   62-4361   F-105B
Known as **YANKEE PEDDLER** with the Kansas Air National Guard. She carried the names **CHRISTIE**, **THE WAR WAGON**, and **BLUE MAX** during her combat service. She is preserved in Columbus, Ohio. (Geer)

641   62-4362   F-105B
Shown in "Look Alike" silver paint. Crashed February 27, 1966, at Takhli due to engine failure. (Geer/Campbell Archive)

642   62-4363   F-105B
Lost December 15, 1965, over RP/6B. Captain Harry Dewitt was rescued.

643   62-4364   F-105B
Written off due to ground accident at Takhli on February 5, 1969. (USAF)

644   62-4365   F-105B
Shown in the colors of the 149th TFS Virginia Air National Guard, in June 1974. Carried the nicknames **PUFF THE MAGIC DRAGON** and **T.C.'S TOY**. (Geer)

645   62-4366   F-105B
Hit by AA over RP1 and crashed in Laos November 4, 1966. Captain Dean Elmer was rescued.

639 ▲

▼ 640   **644▼**

646▲

649 ▲

650▲

▼ 651

646 62-4367   F-105D
Lost to AA fire over RP1 July 14, 1968. Major R.K. Hanna was rescued. (USAF/Robert D. Archer)

647 62-4368   F-105D
Crashed July 13, 1966, at Takhli.

648 62-4369   F-105D
Lost over RP6A, September 4, 1966. Lt. Ronald Bliss ejected to become a POW.

649 62-4370   F-105D
(Foreground) Hit by 100 mm(AAA). Crashed in RP-6A. Lt. Michael L. Brazelton ejected to become a P.O.W. on August 8, 1966. (Minert Collection)

650 62-4371   F-105D
Shot down over RP6 September 21, 1966. Captain G.L. Ammon listed as MIA. (Jay)

651 62-4372   F-105D
Shown in the markings of the 507th TFG she crashed at Tinker AFB August 26, 1981. During her service with the 357th TFS she was known as **THE SUPERSONIC SALAMANDER**. (Goodall)

652 62-4373   F-105D
Hit by AAA over Laos July 24, 1965. Major W.L. McClelland ejected and was rescued.

653 62-4374   F-105D
Crashed May 15, 1965, due to engine failure. She was serving with the 357th TFS at Takhli.

654 62-4375   F-105D
Shown while serving with the 465th TFS, 507th TFG May 3, 1980. During her combat days she carried the name **OLD CROW II** and was the mount of Col. C.E. "Bud" Anderson. She is preserved at Topeka, Kansas. (Minert Collection)

655 62-4376   F-105D
Shot down over RP6B by AAA October 5,1965, during a mission to the Lang Met Bridge. Captain Bruce Seeber escaped the aircraft and was taken POW.

656 62-4377   F-105D
Hit by AAA over RP1 June 15, 1966. Lt. P.J.Kelly was rescued.

657 62-4378   F-105D
Hit by AAA over RP1 August 17, 1967. Major Albert Vollmer nursed the aircraft to the sea and ejected. He was picked up and returned to base. (See 62-4352. 4th on the flightline.)

658 62-4379   F-105D
Shot down November 2, 1966, over RP5. Captain R.F. Loken was rescued. (USAF)

659 62-4380   F-105D
Lost August 1, 1966, over RP6A during a mission to the Thai Nguyen RR Yard. Captain Kenneth North became a POW.

660 62-4381   F-105D
GIVE EM 'L' from the 388th TFW. Lost to groundfire over RP4 May 31, 1965. Lt. Robert Peel captured. (USAF/Robert D. Archer)

661 62-4382   F-105D
First assigned to 8th TFW September 29, 1963. Crashed near Osan AB, Korea, January 31, 1967.

662 62-4383   F-105D
Shown at Tinker AFB April 1978. Preserved at March AFB. (Franklin)

663 62-4384   F-105D
Serving with the Virginia Air National Guard in this photo. She carried the name **BIG RED** while serving with the 333rd TFS, 355th TFW. Later known as **RED RIVER RAIDER.** Crashed near Ft. Bragg, N.C., March 10, 1981, killing Lt/Col. James Gunter, Jr. (Robert Mills, Jr.)

664 62-4385   F-105D
Lost to groundfire over Laos February 28, 1968. Lt/Col. Gene Basel was rescued on this his 79th mission. (USAF/ Robert D. Archer)

665 62-4386   F-105D
Shown while serving with the 563rd TFS, 23rd TFW at Yokota in January 1965. She was lost May 31, 1966, over RP5. Lt. Leonard Ekman ejected and was rescued. (Soldeus)

654 ▲

658 ▲   ▼ 660

662 ▲   ▼ 663

664 ▼

672 ▲

667 ▲

666 62-4387   F-105D
Serving with the Kansas Air National Guard December 7, 1974. She carried the names **SWEET BIPPY, EVE OF DESTRUCTION, DEVIL'S ANGEL/ GRIM REEPER.** She is preserved at Kelly AFB. (Author's Collection)

667 62-4388   F-105D
Crashed February 22, 1966, near Takhli. (USAF/Robert D. Archer) .

668 62-4389   F-105D
Lost due to groundfire September 2, 1965, over RP5. Major J. Quincey Collins was captured.

669 62-4390   F-105D
Crashed March 25, 1964, near Itazuke AB, Japan.

670 62-4391   F-105D
Lost over RP3 October 14, 1966, while on a mission to the Khe Bo Hwy Bridge. Major R.P. Taylor was rescued.

671 62-4392   F-105D
First assigned to the 8th TFW, October 30, 1963. Crashed September 8, 1964.

672 62-4393   F-105D
Hit by groundfire over RP1 June 1, 1966. Captain G.H. Peacock was rescued. (USAF/Robert D. Archer)

665 ▲   ▼ **666**

673▲

675▲

674 ▲

677▼

673 62-4394   F-105D
BIG BUNNY at Korat in 1968. She blew a tire on take off July 16, 1969. The pilot was killed in the crash. Credited with a MiG 17 on October 18, 1967. (Soldeus)

674 62-4395   F-105D
Crashed April 5, 1967, due to drag chute failure. Nicknamed **EMILY**. (USAF)

675 62-4396   F-105D
Shown at Nellis AFB in August 1964. Shot down over RP1 October 27, 1966. Major Dale Johnson listed as KIA. (Isham)

676 62-4397   F-105D
Crashed April 13, 1964, while serving with the 8th TFW at Itazuke AB, Japan.

677 62-4398   F-105D
Crashed July 3, 1965, while serving with the 563rd TFS at Takhli. Crashed was caused by fuel starvation. (Minert Collection)

678　62-4399　F-105D
Shown while serving with the 18th TFW at Kadena. Crashed March 8, 1972, near Kadena. (Meyerson)

679　62-4400　F-105D
Crashed in Thailand due to an in-flight fire September 6, 1965. Photographed with the 4th TFW flying off the left wing of 63-8343. (Malerba)

680　62-4401　F-105D
Lost over RP6A May 5, 1967. Lt/Col James Hughes taken POW. Nicknamed **THE FLYING DUTCHMAN** (See above photo, flying off right wing of 63-8343)

681　62-4402　F-105D
Crashed near Clonmel Kansas June 1, 1964. Captain Billy Sparks ejected.

682　62-4403　F-105D
First assigned to the 388th TFW at McConnell AFB November 22, 1963. Crashed near Kadena September 13, 1967.

683　62-4404　F-105D
She was lost September 28, 1965, due to an in-flight fire. (See 61-0113)

684　62-4405　F-105D
Lost over RP5 May 3, 1967. Major Charles Vasiliadis was rescued. Aircraft was hit in left wing by 37mm groundfire while attacking trucks on the ground.

685　62-4406　F-105D
First assigned to the 388th TFW McConnell AFB November 22, 1963. Crashed near Fallon KS November 18, 1964.

686　62-4407　F-105D
Shot down over RP5 July 27, 1965. Captain F.J. Tullo ejected and was rescued.

687　62-4408　F-105D
Shown in the markings of the 23rd TFW McConnell AFB. Shot down by AA over Laos May 9, 1965. Captain Bob Wistrand KIA. (Minert Collection)

688　62-4409　F-105D
Lost April 22, 1966, over RP6A. Captain Charles Boyd captured. It was his 106th mission.

689　62-4410　F-105D
Lost to groundfire over RP1. Major J.L. Hutto was rescued.

690　62-4411　F-105D
Shown while serving with the 562nd TFS 23rd TFW in June 1972. She carried the name **MAGNET ASP** while serving with the Virginia Air National Guard. She was the last F-105D built.

678▲▼

▼ 679

682▲

687▲   ▼690

▲691   692▲

691   62-4412   F-105F
The prototype F-105F. First assigned to the 4520th CCTW Nellis AFB June 11, 1963. Crashed January 17, 1966. (Minert Collection)

692   62-4413   F-105F
Shown at Eglin AFB in June 1972, in an interesting overall gray paint job. She carried the names **THE FLYING DUTCHMAN, FLYING ANVIL, FLYING ANVIL II**, and **LITTLE DEUCE COUPE**. (Brewer)

693   62-4414   F-105G
Prototype F-105G. Known as **RIDGE RUNNER** while serving with 149th TFS Virginia Air National Guard. (Spering)

694   62-4415   F-105G
DAWN'S DADDY'S RICKIE TICKIE GO-GO CHINE from the 354th TFS, February 1969. She was also known as **SAM SEDUCER** and **NIGHT BIRD**. She crash landed and burned at Takli April 16,1970. (Caldwell)

695   62-4416   F-105G
This was the prototype for the EF-105F "Wild Weasel". She carried the nicknames **LITTLE STEVIE** and **VEGETABLE**. (Miller)

693▲

694▼

695▼

709▲

711▲

712▼

708 62-4429   F-105F
Lost to AAA over RP6 May 15, 1967. Major Ben Pollard and Captain Donald Heiliger taken POW.

709 62-4430   F-105F
Shot down over RP5 on November 5, 1967. Major Richard Dutton and Captain Earl Cobeil taken POW. Captain Cobeil later died in a POW camp. (Chesley)

710 62-4431   F-105F
Crashed April 17, 1964, 50 miles west of Geneva, Switz., near Simaudre, Fr. Aircraft suffered inflight explosion. Crew ejected.

711 62-4432   F-105G
Serving with the 66th FWS, 57th FWW. Modified during the Combat Martin Project to carry a ORC-128 voice jammer in the backseat. (Minert Collection)

712 62-4433   F-105F
Photographed at Andrews AFB July 11, 1975, while serving with the D.C. Air National Guard.(Author's Collection)

713 62-4434   F-105G
Known as **SNAGGLE TOOTH** she was the first F-105F modified to F-105G standards. (Miller)

714 62-4435   F-105F
Photographed in 1964. Carried the nick-name **ROMAN KNIGHT**. Shot down May 14, 1969, over Laos. (Minert Collection)

713▼

714▼

715▲

717▲

715 62-4436 F-105G
On the tankers boom in August 1970.
Lost to AAA November 21, 1970, over
Laos. Major Don Kilgus and Captain
C.T. Lowry were rescued by the Son
Tay Raiders. She carried the name **FAT
FANNY**. (Meyerson)

716 62-4437 F-105F
First assigned to the 4th TFW February 26, 1964. Crashed October 18,
1964, while serving with the 4th TFW.

717 62-4438 F-105G
Shown in the colors of the 352nd TFS
at George AFB. (Minert Collection)

718 62-4439 F-105G
TRUKIN MAMA/HOPELESS on the
Korat flightline in October 1972. (Miller)

719 62-4440 F-105G
ZERO from the 17th WWS, 388thTFW
Korat, Thailand, December 28, 1972.
(Copic)

720 62-4441 F-105F
Crashed at Tahkli January 6, 1968, due
to engine failure.

721 62-4442 F-105G
THE FREEK after her combat service.
Now serving with the Virginia Air National Guard. (MacSorley)

718▲

719▼

721▼

722 ▲

724 ▲

723 ▲

722 62-4443   F-105EG
Damaged by wingman's drop tank during an encounter with a MiG over RP4, July 29, 1972. Major T.J. Coady and Major H.F. Murphy nursed the aircraft out to sea and ejected. They were picked up by friendly forces. (Loomis)

723 62-4444   F-105G
Shown at McConnell AFB. Modified to Combat Martin aircraft carrying the ORC128 jammer. (Loomis)

724 62-4445   F-105F
Shown in the markings of the 354th TFS 355th TFW. She crashed at Tahkli May 2, 1969, due to a loss of engine oil pressure. (Author's Collection)

725 62-4446   F-105G
SNEAKY PETE/SILENT MAJORITY from the 13th TFS, 388th TFW at Korat. Also known as **MOSTES** while serving with the 388th TFW. Shown serving with the 35th TFW. (Minert Collection)

726 62-4447   F-105F
Lost over RP5 April 30, 1967, to a MiG 21. Major Leo Thorsness and Captain Harold Johnson taken POW. (See 63-8267. 447 in on the boom)

727 63-8260   F-105F
Crashed at Korat September 7, 1967, due to engine failure. (Taylor)

725 ▼

727 ▼

▲728   730▲

728   63-8261   F-105F
Shown in the markings of the 419th
TFW, Hill AFB, Utah. Carried the name
LITTLE DARLIN during combat ser-
vice. (Isham)

729   63-8262   F-105F
Lost over RP3 February 18, 1967, after being hit by a SAM. Captain David
Duart and Captain Jay Jensen ejected
to become POWs.

730   63-8263   F-105F
Photographed at Nellis AFB May 1975.
Crashed in Death Valley, California
September 1, 1978.
(Logan)

731   63-8264   F-105F
Serving with the 8th TFW at Kadena.
Crashed April 21, 1964. (USAF/Rob-
ert D. Archer)

732   63-8265   F-105G
NORTHBOUND headed North in Oc-
tober 1972. Scrapped at Torrejon AB,
Spain. (Miller)

733   63-8266   F-105G
Shown in the colors of the 562nd TFS,
36th TFW. She was known as **WHITE
LIGHTNING** while serving with the 17th
WWS at Korat. She is preserved at Lib-
eral, Kansas. (Minert Collection)

732▲

731▼   733▼

734 ▲

735 ▲

741 ▲

739 ▼

738 ▼

734 63-8267   F-105F
Crash landed at Tahkli September 26, 1967. (Chesley)

735 63-8268   F-105F
Photographed at Kadena while serving with the 12th TFS, 18th TFW December 12, 1967. Crashed January 29, 1970, near Osan, Korea. (Miller)

736 63-8269   F-105F
Lost May 12, 1967, over RP1. Captain P.P. Pitman and Captain R.A. Stewart listed as KIA.

737 63-8270   F-105F
Crashed September 7, 1965, near Nellis AFB.

738 63-8271   F-105F
First assigned to the 8th TFW at Itazuke AFB, May 6, 1964. Crashed October 6, 1961, near Hutchison, KS. (Kouda/Robert D. Archer)

739 63-8272   F-105F
Written off October 6, 1967, at Korat due to drag chute failure. (USAF)

740 63-8273   F-105F
Lost to AAA over RP6A November 4, 1966. Major Robert Brinkman and Captain Vince Scungio were killed.

741 63-8274   F-105G
Known as **THE GREAT SPECKLED BIRD** while serving with the 44th TFS. Shown in the colors of the Georgia Air National Guard. (Corry/Isham)

▲743   744▲

742   63-8275   F-105F
NEMESIS on the ramp at Korat in Octo-ber 1972. Also carried the name BONNIE AND CLYDE. (Miller)

743   63-8276   F-105G
Shown while serving with the 562nd TFS, 36th TFW. Known as ANGLE/ BENO BITCH while serving with the 23rd TFW in May 1969. (Minert Collection)

744   63-8277   F-105F
Hit by a SAM over RP5 April 27, 1967. Major John Dudash was killed. Captain Alton Meyer ejected and was taken POW. (Chesley)

745   63-8278   F-105G
Preserved at the California Air National Guard HQ. (USAF/Isham)

746   63-8279   F-105F
Shown in the colors of the 184th TFG. Crashed August 23, 1976, while serving with the 127th TFTS at McConnell AFB, KS. (Isham)

747   63-8280   F-105F
Shown in the lead of this four ship formation. Crashed near Kwangju, Korea, November 5, 1969. (Campbell Archives /OKC)

746▲

747▼

748   63-8281   F-105F
(See above flying right wing) Hit over Laos by AA fire, she crashed in Thailand February 21, 1970. The crew was rescued. She carried the nickname LITTLE ANNIE FANNY while serving with the 388th TFW.

▼745

750▲

▲ 751

752▲

▼ 754

749 63-8282 F-105F
Shot down by AAA over RP5 August 28, 1965. Captain Wesley Schierman taken POW.

750 63-8283 F-105F
First assigned to the 8th TFW at Itazuke May 6, 1964. Crashed July 20, 1968, while serving with the 23rd TFW at McConnell AFB. (Malerba)

751 63-8284 F-105G
GLENNA B/HAZEL BABY of the 357th TFS. Also known as **LYNN'S LA-MENT** and **FREEDOM FIGHTER**. Written off February 2, 1972. (Miller)

752 63-8285 F-105G
Shown in the markings of the 562nd TFS, 36th TFW. She was known as **HONEY**, **PORKY PIG**, and **PEGGY II** during her combat service.(Minert Collection)

753 63-8286 F-105F
Lost to AAA over RP5 July 6, 1966. Major Roosevelt Hestle and Captain Chuck Morgan listed MIA.

754 63-8287 F-105F
Shown while serving with the 465th TFS at Tinker AFB on May 25, 1978. Known as **MISS MARGO/FLAK MAG-NET** while serving with the 354th TFS in January 1970. She made the last operational flight of a THUD on October 28, 1984. She is preserved at Chanute AFB. (Niedermeier/Isham)

755 ▲

756 ▲

755 63-8288   F-105F
Serving with the 561st TFS, 23rd TFW
July 1972. (Miller)

756 63-8289   F-105F
Crashed September 7, 1968, at Korat
due to engine failure. (USAF/Robert D.
Archer)

757 63-8290   F-105F
Crashed at Yokota February 16, 1965.

758 63-8291   F-105G
MUTLEY THE FLYING DOG from the
17th WWS Korat. She was scrapped
at George AFB due to wing cracks. At
one time she was modified to a Combat Martin standard. (Metz)

759 63-8292   F-105G
Shown while serving with the 561st
TFS at Korat in May 1973. (Rotramel)

760 63-8293   F-105F
Hit by AAA over Laos she crashed in
Thailand February 18, 1968. Major
M.S. Muskrat and Captain K. Stouder
were rescued.

761 63-8294   F-105F
Shown in the colors of the Kansas Air
National Guard May 9, 1978. (KAHS)

758 ▲

759 ▼

761 ▼

762▲

MUGLY OTHER

762▲

763▲

762 63-8295   F-105F
Shot down by a MiG 21 over RP5 November 18, 1967, during a mission to the Phuc Yen Airfield. Major O.M. Dardeau was killed in action. Captain E.W. Lehnhoff listed as MIA. Carried the name **MUGLEY OTHER** with the 388th TFW. (Minert Collection)

763 63-8296   F-105G
Photographed at Nellis AFB in April 1980, while serving with the 562nd TFS, 36th TFW. (Norris)

764 63-8297   F-105F
First assigned to the 41st AD at Yokota May 26, 1964. Crashed August 3, 1964.

765 63-8298   F-105F
SAM DODGER leaving Korat for a mission May 29, 1967. Crashed near Kwanju, Korea December 7, 1969. (Isham)

766 63-8299   F-105F
GEORGIA PEACH of the 128th TFS Georgia Air National Guard May 24, 1983. The next day she made the last official flight of a ANG THUD. Her call sign was Peach 91. (Morgan)

765▼

766▼

767   63-8300   F-105G
Preserved at the Le Bourget Museum, Paris. (Author's Collection)

▲ 767   **769 ▲**

768   63-8301   F-105G
Leo Thorsness and Harold Johnson northbound in 301. A historic THUD. Flown by Leo Thorsness on his Medal of Honor mission. She carried the names **THE MOON LIGHTER, JINKIN JOSIE**, and **TAKE HER DOWN**. She was earmarked for the Air Force Museum after her active service. Sadly, she crashed near the Cuddleback Range, California, December 20, 1974. Credited with a MiG 17 during the Medal of Honor mission April 19, 1967. (Chesley)

769   63-8302   F-105G
Known as **HALF A YARD, JEFFERSON AIRPLANE**, and **THE SMITH BROTHERS COUGH DROP SPECIAL**. She was lost to a SAM over RP6A on September 29, 1972. Lt/Col. James O'Neal was taken POW. Captain M.J. Bosiljevac listed as MIA. (Paulson)

770   63-8303   F-105G
Serving with the 562nd TFS. She carried the nickname **NORSK WARRIOR** during her combat service. (Minert Collection)

768 ▲

771   63-8304   F-105G
The **MAD GERMAN EXPRESS** of the 561st TFS, Korat. (Hoynacki)

771 ▼

▼ 768

772▲

773▲

774▲

772 63-8305 F-105G
Serving with the 561st TFS, 388th TFW. (Minert Collection)

773 63-8306 F-105G
Shown in the colors of the 116th TFW April 2, 1982. Known as **BAD SAM**, **TYLER ROSE**, and **PUERTO RICO AIR PIRATE** during her combat service. She was retired to the Aberdeen Proving Ranges. (Minert Collection)

774 63-8307 F-105G
Photographed April 10, 1980, while serving with the 562nd TFS, 35th TFW. (Minert Collection)

775 63-8308 F-105F
Lost to AAA over RP5, August 17, 1966. Major Brand and Major Singer listed as MIA. Shown while serving with the 36th TFW. (Byler)

776 63-8309 F-105F
Stationed at Hill AFB at the time of this photo. She was preserved at Robins AFB, Georgia. (Leavitt/Isham)

777 63-8310 F-105F
Photographed October 14, 1982, serving with the 128th TFS. (Minert Collection)

775▼

776▼

778 63-8311   F-105G
Serving with the 49th TFW May 1966. Crashed November 15, 1970, due to engine failure. Known as **SAM FIGHTER** with the 354th TFS, May 1970. (Geer)

779 63-8312   F-105F
Serving with the 13th TFS at Korat June 23, 1967. Shot down February 29, 1968 over RP6, after being hit by a SAM. Major C.J. Fitton was killed. Captain C.S.Harris listed as MIA. At the time of her loss she was called **MIDNIGHT SUN**. (Isham)

780 63-8313   F-105G
On the ramp at Korat in July 1972 when she was known as **SOD BUSTER**. Also known as **TRUE GRIT**. She was retired to the Aberdeen Ranges after her service. (Hoynacki)

781 63-8314   F-105F
First assigned to the 49th TFW at Spangdahlem. She crashed near Muckeln, Germany, December 12, 1964.

782 63-8315   F-105F
Shown in the colors of the 149th TFS, 192nd TFG Virginia Air National Guard. Crashed near Nicklesville, Georgia, June 4, 1977. (Minert Collection)

783 63-8316   F-105G
From the 355th TFW hooking up with a tanker during a mission. (Meyerson)

▲ 778

779 ▲

780 ▲

▼ 782   783 ▼

784 ▲

▲785

786 ▲

▼787

784   63-8317   F-105F
Photographed while serving with the 13th TFS where she was known as **HALF FAST**. She also carried the name **ROOT PACK RAT**. Lost over RP1 September 30,1968. Credited with a MiG 17 December 19, 1967. (KAHS)

785   63-8318   F-105G
This THUD was modified and served as a Combat Martin aircraft She was written off after a crash landing at Luke AFB January 14, 1976. (Isham)

786   63-8319   F-105G
Northbound while serving with the 17th WWS. Later served with the Georgia Air National Guard. Retired to the Aberdeen Ranges. During her career she carried the names **SAM SEEKER**, **LINDA JEAN**, **SINISTER VAMPIRE TUFFY**, and **HUGGER MUGGER**. (Geer)

787   63-8320   F-105G
The famous **HANOI HUSTLER** leaves the ground for another trip up north. She retired to a place of honor at the Air Force Museum. She also carried the names **BAM BAM**, **COOTER**, and **BABY BEAR'S LAIR**. Although she carries three kill markings there is no documentation as to when these may have occurred. (Minert Collection)

788 63-8321 F-105G
SAWADEE KRUD, September 1972.
Also known as **MISS LUCKY.** Crashed
March 2, 1978, near Newbury Park,
California. (Rotramel)

789 63-8322 F-105F
First assigned to the 36th TFW at
Bitburg. Crashed November 8, 1966.

790 63-8323 F-105F
Crashed August 25, 1968, due to oil
system problems near Takhli.

791 63-8324 F-105F
First assigned to the 36th TFW at
Bitburg. Crashed April 27, 1967 .

792 63-8325 F-105F
Assigned to the 128th TFS, 115th TFG
at the time of this photo. (Grove)

793 63-8326 F-105G
Lost over Laos December 10, 1971. Lt/
Col. S.W. McIntire was killed. Captain
R.E. Belli ejected and was rescued.
(Meyerson)

794 63-8327 F-105G
Headed north to troll for SAMs. Car-
ried the nicknames **SWEET CAR-
OLINE**, **AQUARIUS**, and **PETUNIA
PIG**. She was written off March 12,
1972. (Miller)

795 63-8328 F-105G
Burner blasting out shock diamonds,
she heads out for another mission with
the 66th FWS. (Minert Collection)

796 63-8329 F-105F
Photographed at Da Nang in May
1967. She carried the names
**ROSEMARY'S BABY/PROTEST-
OR'S PROTECTOR**, and **MY DIANE**.
Shot down over Laos/North Vietnam
border January 28, 1972. Captain R.J.
Mallon listed as killed. Captain R.J.
Panek listed MIA. (Geer)

797 63-8330 F-105F
Shot down by a MiG 21 over RP6B
October 6, 1967. Captain J.C. Howard
and Captain G.L. Shamblee nursed the
aircraft out to sea and ejected. They
were picked up.

788▲   ▼ 792

793▼

794▲

▼795

796▼

798 ▲

799 ▲

798 63-8331   F-105F
Photographed June 12, 1973, while serving with the 455th TFS, 507th TFG, at Tinker AFB. (Minert Collection)

799 63-8332   F-105G
Known as **DRAGGIN ASS** during her combat days. She made her last flight on March 17, 1983, when she was retired to the Aberdeen Ranges. (Isham)

800 63-8333   F-105G
Shot down February 17, 1972, over RP1. Captains James Cutter and Kenneth Fraser were taken POW. (USAF/Isham)

801 63-8334   F-105G
From the 17th WWS, 388th TFW at Korat, February 11, 1973. Crashed June 14, 1978, five miles from end of runway at George AFB when engine flamed out. (Isham)

802 63-8335   F-105G
Serving with the 354th TFS at Takhli. Shot down over RP6 on March 10, 1967. Major David Everson and Captain Jose Luna were taken POW. (Geer)

800 ▲

801 ▼

801 ▼

803 ▲

804 ▲

803 63-8336 F-105G
PATIENCE from the 17th WWS, 388th TFW at Korat February 2, 1973.(Isham)

804 63-8337 F-105F
BED CHECK CHARLIE served with the 388th TFW. Shot down April 15, 1968, over RP1. Col. David Winn ejected and was rescued. (Morrison/Isham)

805 63-8338 F-105F
Shot down by a SAM July 23, 1966, over RP6. Major Gene Pemberton and Major Benjamin Newson died in prison camp. (Joe Burch Collection)

806 63-8339 F-105G
Known as **THOR'S HAMMER** and **ROAD RUNNER**. She was retired at Warner Robins, Georgia, and used as a roadside sign for the Museum. (Meyerson)

807 63-8340 F-105G
From the 35th TFW at George AFB. (Sides/Minert)

806 ▲

805 ▼

807▼

808 63-8341   F-105F
Shot down by a MiG over RP6A April 19, 1967. Major Tom Madison and Major Tom Sterling were taken POW. (KAHS)

809 63-8342   F-105G
Serving with the 561st TFW. Shot down by a SAM, April 15, 1972. Captain A.P. Mateja and Captain O.C. Jones Jr were listed as MIA. (Minert Collection)

810 63-8343   F-105F
Photographed during **GOLDFIRE II** in the colors of the 4th TFW, October-November 1964. Reported to be in the process of being restored to flying status by Serria Hotel, at Addison Airport, TX. (USAF/Isham)

811 63-8344   F-105F
Crashed March 4, 1965, near Salina, KS. Crew ejected.

812 63-8345   F-105G
Serving with the 17th WWS at Korat heading north on another mission. Displayed as 62-4425 at Robbins AFB, GA. (Minert Collection)

813 63-8346   F-105F
Lost to groundfire October 5, 1967, during a mission to the Lang Con RR Bridge. Major M.L. McDaniel and Captain W.A. Lillund listed as MIA.

814 63-8347   F-105G
MT IDA FLASH/HONKEY TONK WOMAN photographed in May 1970, while serving with the 44th TFS, 355th TFW. Written off May 17, 1972, after a tire blew. Carried the nickname **DRAGON II** while serving with the 388th TFW at Korat in 1968. (Miller)

815 63-8348   F-105F
Crashed at Yakota AFB May 5, 1968, while TDY from McConnell AFB.

816 63-8349   F-105F
Captain Arnold Dolejsi and his "Bear" Captain Paul Chesley northbound on a mission. Hit by a SAM over RP6A November 19, 1967. Major Gerald Gustafson and Captain Russell Brownlee nursed the aircraft into Laos and ejected. They were rescued. (Chesley)

817 63-8350   F-105G
On approach March 21, 1974, while serving with the 57th TFW. Written off May 1979. (Minert Collection)

808▲   ▼ 809

810▼

812▲ ▼816

814▲ ▼816

817▼

818 63-8351   F-105G
TDY TOO from the 561st TFS at Korat in February 1973. She was written off at George AFB June 10, 1976, due to cracks in the wing. (Metz)

819 63-8352   F-105F
Nicknamed **RAMP TRAMP** and **MR. FLAK BAIT**, she was a historic THUD. Flown by Major Merlyn Dethlefsen, March 10, 1967. For his actions that day he was awarded the Medal of Honor. The aircraft crash landed at Udorn after being hit by AAA December 8, 1969. (Minert Collection)

820 63-8353   F-105F
Lost over RP1, July 15, 1968. Major Gobel James ejected to become a POW. Captain L.E Martin was killed in action. Nick-named **BILLIE FERN/ THUNDERCHIEF**. (USAF/Robert D. Archer)

821 63-8354   F-105F
Crashed at Takhli December 17, 1966, due to engine problems.

822 63-8355   F-105G
Taking off from Nellis for another training mission. (Isham)

823 63-8356   F-105F
MISS MOLLY, shot down by a MiG 17 January 5, 1968, during a mission to the Dong Luc RR Bridge. Major J.C. Hartney listed MIA. Captain S. Fantle III was killed in action. (Chesley)

824 63-8357   F-105F
Photographed July 11, 1975, while serving with the 121st TFS D.C. National Guard. (Minert Collection)

825 63-8358   F-105F
Hit by a SAM over RP6B August 7, 1966. Captain Larsen managed to get the aircraft out to sea were he and Captain K.A. Gilroy ejected and were rescued.

818▲   ▼ 820

819▼

822 ▲

▼ 823

824 ▼

826   63-8359   F-105G
On the Korat ramp October 1972 while serving with the 17th WWS. Shot down by a SAM over RP3 November 16, 1972. (Miller)

827   63-8360   F-105G
Hit by a SAM over RP-6 September 17, 1972. Crashed at sea killing the crew. (Geer)

828   63-8361   F-105F
Lost to AAA fire over RP6B August 7, 1966. Captain Robert Sandvick and Captain Thomas Pyle III ejected and were captured.

829   63-8362   F-105F
Serving with the Virginia Air National Guard August 1978. While serving with this unit she carried the name **DO IT WITH....FINESSE**. (KAHS)

830   63-8363   F-105G
Photographed while serving with the Georgia Air National Guard in April 1980. (Leader)

831   63-8364   F-105F
Serving with the 18th TFW at Kadena January 9, 1965. Crashed July 23, 1966, at Fairchild AFB, WA. (Republic)

832   63-8365   F-105F
THE DIRTY DUCK from 466th TFS, 508th TFW at Hill AFB, Utah. (Isham)

833   63-8366   F-105F
The last F-105 built. She is preserved at McConnell AFB. At one time she carried the name **MISS MOLLY 2**. Note the unit crest of the 384th BW on the tail. (KAHS)

826▲

▼827

830▼

831▲

▼ 832

833▼

THUD ART

Aircraft have carried artwork into combat since the first two aerial adversaries shot at each other with pistols. The F-105 was no exception to the rule. The names she carried during her service career reflected not only her mission but the politics and feelings of the time. Names like PROTESTOR'S PROTECTOR, NORTHBOUND and THE SILENT MAJORITY adorned her sides commenting on the war that was being run from the "White House".

The reason for an individual name being placed on the side of a THUD was as varied as the men who flew and maintained them. For whatever the reason, they appeared with or without official sanction. These names gave an otherwise large collection of aluminum parts resembling an F-105 a unique personification.

Many of these examples of artwork ended as smoldering hulks somewhere in the jungles or rice paddies of Southeast Asia. We remember these aircraft through the photographs that were taken during their service.

Artwork and names for the F-105 appeared in three basic locations. The first was on the edge of the intake. The second was on the fuselage below the cockpit. The last area was just under the intake and makes up an area that for lack of a better name was called "armpit art".

It is impossible to show every example of artwork that appeared on the F-105s. We can only hope that this brief sampling will wet your whistle for more and more THUD ART.

F-105B (57-5835) carried the name BROOKS BARN STORMER in this August 1981 photo. (Kern)

The Thai spelling of Captain Jim Boyd's wife became KLOYJAI. Photo taken in October 1972. (Metz)

WHITE LIGHTNING (63-8266) was a "Wild Weasel" from the 17th WWS at Korat in February 1973. (Metz)

MUTLEY THE FLYING DOG (63-8291), another Wild Weasel at Korat in February 1973 . (Metz)

F-105D 60-0488 was known as AQUARIUS while serving with 44th TFS, 355th TFW at Takhli.

With six SAM site "Kills" to her credit SAM FIGHTER (63-8311) seems to live up to her name. She was serving with the 354th TFS in this May 1970 photo. (Metz)

PATIENCE MY ASS (61-0176) from the 357th TFW in April 1969. (Caldwell)

Loaded for her next trip up north THE IMPOSSIBLE DREAM (62-4269) evokes the feelings that the end of the tour is an impossible dream. (Fitzharris)

During her combat days 62-4387 carried the name DEVIL'S ANGEL. When she returned to the states she was assigned to the Kansas Air National Guard. The new crew chief painstakingly removed the over cover of paint to expose the old artwork. (Campbell Archives/OKC)

Flown by Captain Peter Foley on his 200 combat mission she was known as FOLEY'S FOLEY. (Campbell)

This artwork appeared on the right side of 59-1771 otherwise known as FOLEY'S FOLEY.(USAF/Robert D. Archer)

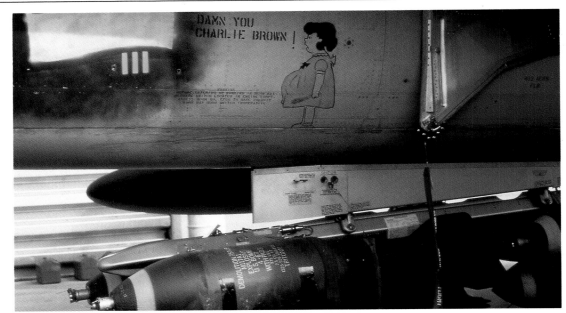

Loaded for the next mission in more ways than one. DAMN YOU CHARLIE BROWN wore serial number 60-0434. (Campbell Archives/OKC)

Serving with the 562nd TFS, 357th TFW in July 1980, 62-4416 was known as SAM SLAYER. Note the six kill markings under the canopy. (Minert Collection)

HOPELESS (62-4439) from the 561st TFS. (Metz)

(TA-14) Stationed at Korat in January 1973, BUF'S BUDDY carried serial number 62-4422. (Metz)

She carried several names. THE MOONLIGHTER, TAKE HER DOWN are two examples. In June 1968 she was known as JINKIN JOSIE. Underneath the artwork she was 63-8301, the aircraft that Leo Thorsness flew his Medal of Honor mission in. (Pepperill)

SUZY BABY (61-0165) from the 357th TFS in February 1969. (Caldwell)

TA-17) SITTING PRETTY (61-0078) served with the 469th TFS, 388th TFW.

Carrying the name of a popular movie, BONNIE AND CLYDE (63-8275) served with the 44th TFS, 388th TFW in August 1968. (USAF/Robert D. Archer)

BUTTERFLY BOMBER (60-0423) flew with the 44th TFS.

F-105D 60-0432 was known as FARTIN MARTIN.

MR BLACKBIRD (61-0205) ready for another mission while serving with the 34th TFS.

BUNNY BABY (60-0409) flew from Korat during her combat service.

DEE DEE II (60-0464). Later she was known as M.J. with the 355th TFW.

Rather suggestive artwork on (61-0069) serving with the 80th TFS, 8th TFW at Takhli in 1966. At that time she carried the name PUSSY GALORE. (Mikesh)

The artwork on PUSSY GALORE was spared when she went through the paint shop to have her new warpaint applied. (Mikesh)

BILLIE BABE , 60-0518, served with the 469th TFS at Korat.

THE GREAT SPECKLED BIRD (63-8274) served with the 44th TFS, 388th TFW. It was said she had the ability to "molt" her paint like feathers on a bird. (USAF/Robert D. Archer)

RUM RUNNER (62-4428) from the 44th TFS, 388th TFW in July 1968. (USAF/Robert D. Archer)

YANKEE AIR PIRATE (60-0453) ready for another mission.

Two red cherries adorned the side of 63-8363 while serving with the 44th TFS, 388th TFW. (USAF/Robert D. Archer)

This THUD was called THE PINK PUSSY and was most likely a play on the movie PINK PANTHER.

A rather appropriate name for a THUD. FOREIGN AID (61-0219) in June 1968. Later she carried the name THE TRAVELER. (Kamm/Robert D. Archer)

ARKANSAS RAZORBACK (58-1152) from the 388th TFW. (USAF/Robert D. Archer)

ANGEL was under the left wing while THE BENO BITCH reclined under the right wing of 63-8276 from the 388th TFW in May 1969. (USAF/Robert D. Archer)

THE VIRGINIAN (63-8336) from the 44th TFS, 388th TFW. (USAF/Robert D. Archer)

This tiger adorned 60-0428 from the 469th TFS, 388th TFW. (USAF/Robert D. Archer)

GOOD GOLLY MISS MOLLY (62-4346) from the 469th TFS, 388th TFW, in June 1966. In May 1962 she was known as ITAZUKE EXPRESS. (USAF/Robert D. Archer)

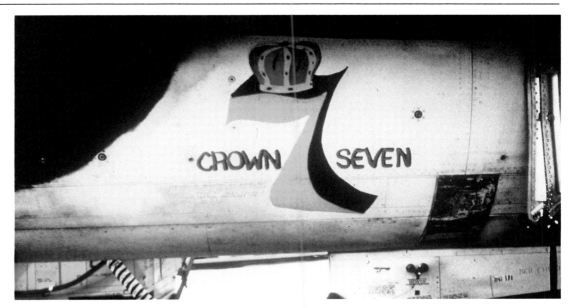

CROWN SEVEN (62-4424) served with the 388th TFS, 388th TFW in June 1968. (USAF/Robert D. Archer)

Without a doubt one of the all-time favorites. NOLI NON LEGITIME CARBOR UNDUM EST (62-4270. Translated to read, "Don't Let The Bastards Wear You Down". She served with the 34th TFS, 388th TFW at Korat. (USAF/Robert D. Archer)

A comment on what was happening back home in the states. THE PROTESTOR'S PROTECTOR (63-8329) flew with the 44th TFS, 388th TFW in February 1968.(USAF/Robert D. Archer)

ROMAN KNIGHT (62-4435) from the
44th TFS, 388th TFW in June 1968.
(USAF/Robert D. Archer)

FREEDOM FIGHTER (63-8284) from
the 388th TFW July 1968. (USAF/Rob-
ert D.Archer)

This F-105 (60-0513) carried this artwork to boneyard with the message
that when she was cut apart the artwork was to be returned to Carswell
AFB, Texas.

TOP DOG (60-0498) served with the 149th TFS Virginia Air National Guard. (Campbell Archives/OKC)

MY KARMA (62-0301) stationed at Hill AFB. (Minert Collection)

KOMBAT KATHY (61-0108) from the 466th TFS.

SILVER TONGUE DEVIL (62-4228) from the 466th TFS, 508th TFG May 8,1983. (Gaston)

MILLARD THE MALLARD (61-0167) served with the Virginia Air National Guard. (Campbell Archives/OKC)

FLYING ANVIL (62-4413) from the Virginia Air National Guard. (Muir)

Serving with the 149th TFS, 192nd TFG Virginia Air National Guard. Under the REAGLE BEAGLE artwork she was 61-0071. (Swendrowski)

THUNDER AX (61-0170) from the Virginia Air National Guard. She obtained this name after she clipped three trees and a power pole during a very low level pass. (Campbell Archives/OKC)

YE OLD WAR HORSE (60-0492) served her final days with the Virginia Air National Guard. (Campbell Archives/OKC)

Rocky and Bullwinkle joined the Virginia Air National Guard to become DYNAMIC DUO on 59-1771. She was also known as FOLEY'S FOLLY/OHIO EXPRESS and UNDERDOG II. (Minert Collection)

Commenting on their role as Wild Weasels, DO IT WITH FINESSE (63-8363) served with the Virginia Air National Guard. (Campbell Archives/OKC)

In 1980 she was RED RIVER RAIDER(62-4384) while serving with the 149th TFS, 192nd TFG. She went "Downtown" many times as BIG RED with the 355th TFW in 1970.(Minert Collection)

REBEL RIDER (60-0452) from the 149th TFS, Virginia ANG. (Campbell Archives/OKC)

Commenting on her past service, HANOI EXPRESS served with the Virginia Air Guard. During her combat service she was known as LEAD ZEPPELIN, ARKANSAS TRAVELER, and DARN DAGO. She is preserved at Hill AFB in the colors of ARKANSAS TRAVELER. (Isham)

F-105 59-1822 carried the name SUPERHOG with the 149th TFS. While serving with the 44th TFS, 388th TFW she was known as THE POLISH GLIDER. (Swendrowski)

KILLER ACE (62-4418) from the 149th TFS, Virginia Air National Guard. (Isham)

RIDGE RUNNER (62-4414) 149TH TFS, VANG traces her past to running along THUD RIDGE just north of Hanoi. (Campbell Archives/OKC)

With 6,730 flying hours she earned the name HIGH TIME THUD.

Although she was the HIGH TIME THUD, she (62-4347) was also known as STAR DUST 6 while serving with the 466th TFS out of Hill AFB, Utah.

DESERT FOX (62-4299) took her name from her desert style paint job. She was part of the Air Force Reserve at Hill, AFB.

KUKHUI was photographed at Nellis AFB in June 1983. (Minert Collection)

BATTLIN GATLIN (62-4344) in the Virginia Air Guard in May 1980. She was known as RITA BABY in June 1969. Later she was called WELFARE CADILLAC/WYOMING THUD while serving with the 355th TFW. (Swendrowski)

FLYING ANVIL IV (59-1750) attests to the loss rate over targets. She served with the 469th TFS.

This nice artwork went with QUEEN OF THE FLEET (59-1739) She carried the same name with different artwork while serving with the 388th TFW. (Minert Collection)

61-0164 was known as GOLDEN GUN with the Virginia Air National Guard.

THUNDERCHIEF (61-0212) Virginia Air Guard. During her combat service she carried names like PEACE EN-VOY and RUNNING GUN V.

THE DIRTY DUCK (63-8365) from the 466th TFS. (Minert Collection)

In 1970 she was known as FRITO BANDITO with the 357th TFS. Her combat days over she served with the Virginia Air Guard as HUN'S HAMMER. (Campbell Archives/OKC)

This provocative artwork adorned the side of MY HONEYPOT in 1980. She carried serial number 61-0145. (Bailey)

KEEP EM FLYING (61-0086) from the Virginia Air National Guard. (Minert Collection)

MAGNET ASP (62-4411) from the 149th TFS. (Campbell Archives/OKC)

HAVE GUN WILL TRAVEL (61-0159) 192nd TFG (VANG). She carried the same name during her combat service with the 355th TFW in January 1970. (Minert Collection)

F-105F (63-8261) BOSS HOSS. (Campbell Archives/OKC)

NO GUTS NO GLORY from the 466th TFS July 1982. (Campbell Archives/ OKC)

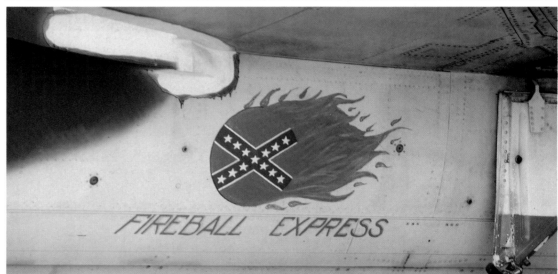

Serving with the 149th TFS VANG in June 1980. FIREBALLEXPRESS carried serial number 60-5385.(Campbell Archives/OKC)

THUD ART is not restricted to the sides of the airplane. Sometimes artwork appears on the GCA antenna. This artwork was photographed on a THUD at George AFB, July 1980. (Minert Collection)

PATIENCE MY ASS, I'M GONNA KILL SOMETHING was found on 60-0504, while serving with the 121st TFS, 133rd TFG. (Minert Collection)

This nice artwork adorned an unknown THUD. (Campbell Archives/OKC)

THE BOSS (58-1150) served with the 388th TFS at Korat. (USAF/Robert D. Archer)

60-0505 carried this artwork while serving with the 388th TFW. On the nose wheel door was inscribed THE 25 TON CANARY. (USAF/Robert D. Archer)

ARKANSAS TRAVELLER (59-1743) was the personal mount of Colonel Paul Douglas of the 388th TFW. This aircraft is preserved at Hill AFB, Utah. (USAF/Robert D. Archer)

DON'T TREAD ON ME (61-0086) flew with the 388th TFW. (USAF/Robert D. Archer)

Another 388th TFW THUD was SCHMOO'S MAGOO (60-0488). (USAF/Robert D. Archer)

The artwork on 61-0220, stemmed from a popular TV show I DREAM OF JEANIE. She was assigned to the 388th TFW in 1968. (USAF/Robert D. Archer)

LADY LUCK carried serial number 62-4248 and flew with the 388th TFW. (USAF/Robert D. Archer)

BIG MIKE (62-4269) from the 388th TFW at Korat. (USAF/Robert D> Archer)

12 O'CLOCK HIGH (62-4360) from the 469th TFS, 388th TFW at Korat. (USAF)

In January 1970 61-0159 was known as HONEY POT II/HAVE GUN WILL TRAVEL while serving with the 354th TFS, 355th TFW at Takhli. (USAF)

Perhaps commenting on her green and tan paint job SUPERSONIC SALAMANDER (62-4372) served with the 357th TFS, 355th TFW at Takhli in January 1970. (USAF)

THE FRITO BANDITO (59-1731) was the personal mount of Major Joe Olvera from the 357th TFS, 355th TFW in January 1970. (USAF)

Serving with the 357th TFS, 355th TFW in January 1968 she was called DAISEY MAE (58-1172). (USAF)

THE BALD EAGLE (60-5375) was the personal mount of Colonel Heath Bottomly of the 333rd TFS, 355th TFW June 1969. (USAF)

PAPA THUD/MUTT'S MAN-O-WAR (62-4228) from the 354th TFS, 355th TFW at Takhli in January 1970.(USAF)

The TAKHLI TAXI (59-1729) from the 333rd TFS, 355th TFW at Takhli in January 1970. (USAF)

BIG RED (62-4384) ready for another mission up north. She was serving with the 333rd TFS, 355th TFW at Takhli in January 1970. (USAF)

Major R. Rogers flew THE JOLLY ROGER (61-0176) while serving with the 357th TFS, 355th TFW in January 1970. (USAF)

DRAGON III flew with the 388th TFW in 1968. (USAF/Robert D. Archer)

THE JEFFERSON AIRPLANE from the 388th TFW at Korat circa 1968. (USAF/Robert D. Archer)

MY BITT II was assigned to the 388th TFW. (USAF/Robert D. Archer)

ROMANS 8:31 appeared on the nose wheel door of I DREAM OF JEANIE (61-0220) at Korat. (USAF/Robert D. Archer)

Serial number 61-0194 carried the name THE AVENGER II into combat during her service with the 388th TFW. (USAF/Robert D. Archer)

THE OUTLAW (61-0161) served at Korat during 1968. (USAF/Robert D. Archer)

Another THUD from Korat, this time she is BETTY LOU (61-0086). (USAF/Robert D. Archer)

When the Wild Weasels got a valid launch signal they would call TAKE HER DOWN. This is actually 63-8301 better known as JINKIN JOSIE, THE MOONLIGHTER. Compare the artwork as it appears here with JINKIN JOSIE. (USAF)

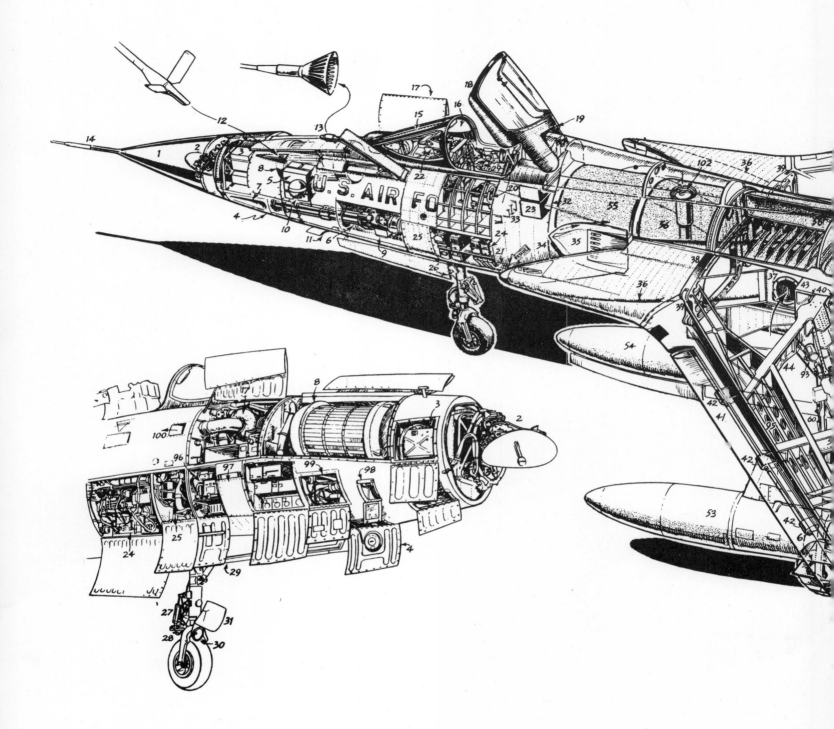

REPUBLIC F-105D...